D1330309

ONE WEEK LOAN

1 2 OCT 2010

THE WEST
AND
THE REST

GLOBALIZATION AND THE
TERRORIST THREAT

ROGER SCRUTON

 continuum
LONDON • NEW YORK

Continuum
The Tower Building
11 York Road
London SE1 7NX
www.continuumbooks.com

370 Lexington Avenue
New York
NY 10017-6503

First published in 2002, reprinted in 2002, 2003

British Library Cataloguing-in-Publication Data
A catalogue record for this book is available from the British Library.

ISBN 0-8264-6496-3 (Hardback)
ISBN 0-8264-7030-0 (Paperback)

U.S. Cataloguing-in-Publication Data
Scruton, Roger
    The west and the rest; globalization and the terrorist threat/
    Roger Scruton. – 1st ed. – Wilmington, Del.: ISI Books, 2002

    p. ; cm
    Includes index

ISBN 1-882926-81-1
    1. Globalization. 2. Globalization – Religious aspects. 3.
    Religion and international affairs. 4. International relation. 5.
    Terrorism. I. Title. II. Globalization and the terrorist threat.

JZ1318.S37 2002   2002107924
291.1787–dc21   0209

Interior book design by Sam Torode
Printed and bound by The Bath Press

CONTENTS

PREFACE

SAMUEL HUNTINGTON'S celebrated thesis that the Cold War has been succeeded by a "clash of civilizations" has more credibility today than it had in 1993, when it was first put forward.[1] For many observers, reflecting on the calamity of September 11, the world has divided into two spheres—the sphere of freedom and democracy, and the sphere of despotism, "failed states," and religious zeal. This reverses the familiar Islamic division, between the *dar al-islam* and the *dar al-harb*: the house of submission and the house of war. And it reflects a habit of mind against which Huntington and others have warned. Western "universalism," as Huntington calls it, sees the whole world in terms of values that have their origin, meaning, and natural climate in what is in fact only a small (though admittedly noisy) part of it. To transfer those values to places that have been deeply inoculated against them by culture and custom is to invite the very confrontation that we seek to avoid.

Others write of Western decadence and loss of direction, implying that our civilization lacks the spiritual and moral resources to defend itself against the new terrorist threat. But, apart from the vague reference to Spengler and Toynbee contained in the word "Western," very little thought has been expended on what seems to me to be the real question: What exactly is Western civilization, and what holds it together? Politicians, asked to define what we are fighting for in the "war against terrorism," will always say freedom. But, taken by itself, freedom means the emancipation from constraints, including those constraints which might be needed if a civilization is to endure. If *all* that Western civilization offers is freedom, then it is a civilization bent on its own destruction. Moreover freedom flaunted in the face of religious prohibitions is an act of aggression, inviting retribution from those whose piety it offends.

Islamic civilization involves a common religious belief, based on a sacred text whose law may be misapplied but never altered. It defines itself in terms not of freedom but of submission. *Islam*, *salm,* and *salaam*—"submission," "peace," and "safety"—all derive from the verb *salima*, whose primary meaning is "to be secure," "unharmed," or "blameless," but which has a derived form meaning "to surrender."[2] The *muslim* is the one who has surrendered, submitted, and so obtained security. In that complex etymological knot is tied a vision of society and its rewards far different from anything that has prevailed in modern

Europe and America.

Western civilization also grew from a common religious belief and a sacred text, and, like Islam, originated in a religious movement among Semitic people—albeit people living under an imperial yoke, for whom submission was already a day-to-day reality. Western civilization has left behind its religious belief and its sacred text, to place its trust not in religious certainties but in open discussion, trial and error, and the ubiquitousness of doubt. But the odd thing is that, while Islamic civilization is riven by conflict, Western civilization seems to have a built-in tendency to equilibrium. Freedoms that Western citizens take for granted are all but unheard of in Islamic countries, and while no Western citizens are fleeing from the West, 70 percent of the world's refugees are Muslims fleeing from places where their religion is the official doctrine. Moreover, those refugees are all fleeing to the West, recognizing no other place as able to grant the opportunities, freedoms, and personal safety that they despair of finding at home.

Equally odd, however, is the fact that, having arrived in the West, many of these Muslim refugees begin to conceive a hatred of the society by which they find themselves surrounded, and aspire to take revenge against it for some fault so heinous that they can conceive of nothing less than final destruction as the fitting punishment. Odder still is the fact that those Muslims who settle down, integrate, and acquire some kind of loyalty to Western institutions and customs often produce children who, despite being brought up in the West, identify themselves in opposition to it—an opposition so fierce as again to verge on the desire for annihilation.

A superficial response to these disturbing facts is to put the blame on Islam—to argue, with an undeniable degree of plausibility, that Islam is a medieval fossil, unadapted to modern conditions, and unable to adjust to the enormous social, economic, and demographic changes that have shaken our planet. But then "modern conditions" are precisely those conditions which result from the global outreach of Western technology, Western institutions, and Western conceptions of political freedom. Why blame Islam for rejecting them, when they, in their turn, involve a rejection of the idea on which Islam is founded—the idea of God's immutable will, revealed once and for all to his Prophet, in the form of an unbreachable and unchangeable code of law?

In this book I explore the vision of society and political order that lies at the heart of "Western civilization." And I try to show how the apparent conflict with Islam is fed by the decay of that vision, and the loss of the political loyalty on which it depends. When distinguishing "the rest" from the West I do not mean to imply that there is a unified antipathy to the Western way of life, or that the world is divided into opposing camps, as perhaps it was during the Cold War. However, it seems to me that there is a great difference between those parts where the Western political project has taken root, and those where it has not. I focus on Islam, since it offers such a clear alternative to that project, one with a history of successes as well as failures. Today the failures prevail: and this is one source of our present danger. For failure is no longer localized in the place that produced it, but carries its burden of resentment around the world.

My theme in what follows is not historical; nor do I deal in any depth with the movements or individuals that occupy the stage of modern politics. My concern is primarily conceptual: to understand the kinds of order and disorder that emerge when the resources and techniques of modern life are severed from the political process that might otherwise control them—the political process that defines what is known as the "West."

— *Malmesbury, spring 2002*

CHAPTER I

THE SOCIAL CONTRACT

THE WORD "RELIGION" derives from the Latin *religio*, the root of which, according to a disputed ancient tradition, is *ligere*, "to bind." Looked at from the outside, religions are defined by the communities who adopt them, and their function is to bind those communities together, to secure them against external shock, and to guarantee the course of reproduction. A religion is founded in piety, which is the habit of submitting to divine commands. This habit, once installed, underpins all oaths and promises, gives sanctity to marriage, and upholds the sacrifices that are needed both in peace and in war. Hence communities with a shared religion have an advantage in the fight for land, and all the settled territories of our planet are places where some dominant religion has at some time staked out and defended its claims.

But religion is not the only form of social binding. There is also politics, by which I mean the government of a community by man-made laws and human decisions, without reference to divine commands. Religion is a static condition; politics a dynamic process. Whereas religions demand unquestioning submission, the political process offers participation, discussion, and lawmaking founded in consent. So it has been in the Western tradition, and at least one thinker has seen the contest between the religious and the political forms of social order as the process that formed the modern world.[1]

However, the contest between religion and politics is not in itself a modern one. This we know not only from the Bible, but also from Greek tragedy. The action of Sophocles' *Antigone* hinges on the conflict between political order, represented and upheld by Creon, and religious duty, represented in the person of Antigone. The first is public, involving the whole community; the second is private, involving Antigone alone. Hence the conflict cannot be resolved. Public interest has no bearing on Antigone's decision to bury her dead brother, while the duty laid by divine command on Antigone cannot possibly be a reason for Creon to jeopardize the state.

A similar conflict informs the *Oresteia* of Aeschylus, in which a succession of religious murders, beginning with Agamemnon's ritual sacrifice of his daughter, lead at last to the terrifying persecution of Orestes by the furies. The gods demand the murders; the gods also punish them. Religion binds the house of Atreus, but in dilemmas that it does not resolve. Resolution comes at last only when judgment is handed over to the city, personified in Athena. In the political order, we are led to understand, justice replaces vengeance, and negotiated solutions abolish absolute commands. The message of the *Oresteia* resounds down the centuries of Western civilization: it is through politics, not religion, that peace is secured. Vengeance is mine, saith the Lord; but justice, says the city, is mine.

The Greek tragedians wrote at the beginning of Western civilization. But their world is continuous with our world. Their law is the law of the city, in which political decisions are arrived at by discussion, participation, and dissent. It was in the context of the Greek city-state that political philosophy began, and the great questions of justice, authority, and the constitution are discussed by Plato and Aristotle in terms that are current today.

However, two great institutions intervene between the modern world and its premonition in ancient Greece: Roman law, conceived as a universal jurisdiction, and Christianity, conceived as a universal church. St. Paul, who transformed the ascetic and self-denying religion of Christ into an organized form of worship, was a Roman citizen, versed in the law, who shaped the early church through the legal idea of the *universitas* or corporation. The Pauline church was designed, not as a sovereign body, but as a universal citizen, entitled to the protection of the secular and imperial powers but with no claim to displace those powers as the source of legal order. This corresponds to Christ's own vision; in his parable of the tribute money, Caesar's public jurisdiction is tacitly contrasted with the inner authority of religion, governing the person-to-person relationship between the individual and God: "Render therefore to Caesar the things that are Caesar's; and unto God the things that are God's" (Matthew 22:21). And it contrasts radically with the vision set before us in the Koran, according to which sovereignty rests with God and his Prophet, and legal order is founded in divine command.

The Christian separation of religious and secular authority recalls Aeschylus's solution to the dilemmas thrust upon mortals by the gods. This Christian approach was developed by St Augustine in *The City of God* and endorsed by the fifth-century *Pastoral Rule* of St Gregory, which imposed the duty of civil obedience on the clergy. The fifth-century Pope Gelasius I made the separation of church and state into doctrinal orthodoxy, arguing that God granted "two swords" for earthly government: that of the Church for the government of men's souls, and that of the imperial power for the regulation of temporal affairs.[2] This idea persists in the medieval distinction between *regnum* and *sacerdotium*, and was enshrined in the uneasy coexistence of Emperor and Pope on the two "universal" thrones of medieval Europe. Much wise and subtle argument was expended by medieval thinkers on the distinction between the two sources of authority in human affairs, with the early fourteenth-century thinker Marsilius of Padua expressing what was to become the accepted Western view of the matter in his *Defensor Pacis*. According to Marsilius it is the state and not the church that guarantees the civil peace, and reason, not revelation, to which appeal must be made in all matters of temporal jurisdiction.

With the breakdown of papal jurisdiction and the rise of the Reformed churches, ecclesiastical law had less and less influence on the business of government. This result did not come about without conflict, and in several cases (England being the most striking instance) there resulted an explicitly "national" church, under the authority of a secular monarch. Nevertheless, throughout the course of Christian civilization we find a recognition that conflicts must be resolved and social order maintained by political rather than religious jurisdiction. The separation of church and state was from the beginning an accepted doctrine of the church. Indeed, this separation *created* the church, which emerged from the Dark Ages as a legal subject, with rights, privileges, and a domestic jurisdiction of its own. And it was through his theory of conciliar government that Nicholas of Cusa, in 1433, introduced the modern understanding of corporate personality, and made it fundamental to our understanding of the church.

No similar institution exists in Islamic countries. There is no legal entity called "The Mosque" to set beside the various Western churches.[3] Nor is there any human institution whose role it is to confer "holy orders" on its members. Those Muslims who have religious authority—the *'ulama'* ("those with knowledge")—possess it directly from God. And those who take on the function of the *imam* ("the one who stands in front"), so leading the congregation in prayer, are often self-appointed to this role. Islam has never incorporated itself as a legal person or a subject institution, a fact that has had enormous political repercussions. Like the Communist Party in its Leninist construction, Islam aims to control the state without being a subject of the state.

Freedom of conscience requires secular government. But what makes secular law legitimate? That question is the starting point of Western political philosophy, and is now mired in academic controversy. But, to cut an interminable story indecently short, the consensus among modern thinkers is that the law is made legitimate by the consent of those who must obey it. This consent is shown in two ways: by a real or implied "social contract," whereby each person agrees with every other to the principles of government; and by a political process through which each person participates in the making and enacting of the law. The right and duty of participation is what we mean, or ought to mean, by "citizenship," and the distinction between political and religious communities can be summed up in the view that the first are composed of citizens, the second of subjects.

This account of legitimacy may not be endorsed by every Western philosopher. But it is endorsed by almost every Western politician, at least when out of office. There seems to be no better justification for imposing a decision on a group of people than to show that the decision is theirs. The social contract and the participatory process are envisaged as mechanisms for transforming the choices of members into the choice of the group. And what better guarantee can I have that a choice made in my name is legitimate than that I myself have made it?

It is for this reason that politicians, asked to define what they mean by the "West," and what the "war against terrorism" is supposed to be defending, will invariably mention freedom as the fundamental idea. Without freedom there cannot be government by consent; and it is the freedom to participate in the process of government, and to protest against, dissent from, and oppose the decisions that are made in my name, that confer on me the dignity of citizenship. Put very briefly, the difference between the West and the rest is that Western societies are governed by politics; the rest are ruled by power.

The idea of the social contract helps us to see both the strengths of Western systems of government and their weaknesses. Although the social contract exists in many forms, its ruling principle was announced by Hobbes, with the assertion that there can be "no obligation on any man which ariseth not from some act of his own."[4] My obligations are my own creation, binding because freely chosen. When you and I exchange promises, the resulting contract is freely undertaken, and any breach does violence not merely to the other but also to the self, since it is a repudiation of a well-grounded rational choice. If we could construe our obligation to the state on the model of a contract, therefore, we would have justified it in terms that all rational beings must accept. Contracts are the paradigms of self-chosen obligations—obligations that are not imposed, commanded, or coerced but freely undertaken. When law is founded in a social contract, therefore, obedience to the law is simply the other side of free choice. Freedom and obedience are one and the same. This was the thought that so excited Rousseau, and the thought Kant was to develop into a comprehensive theory of secular morality.

Contracts create vetoes. If there is a party to an arrangement who cannot agree to its terms, then the contract will be void. Another way of seeing the social contract, therefore, is as a device that endows the ordinary citizen with a veto. Laws to which the citizen cannot consent are illegitimate, and the state must therefore be maintained in a constant state of vigilance, lest it lose the consent of the citizen and the right to command him. A state founded on a social contract is therefore maximally respectful of the autonomy, freedom, and dignity of the individual. Those things which no rational being can agree to surrender—life, limb, and conscience—become, in the contractarian view of things, absolute entitlements or "human rights." And when communities find their happiness and neighborliness through their distinctive ways of life, these too must be protected, by guaranteeing the rights of acknowledged minorities.

The contractarian view of legitimacy takes a decisive step away from the religious conception of the world. Even if I believe that the state was divinely ordained, and that

God's commandments already incline me to civil obedience, it is not this which endows the law with its legitimacy. For my fellow citizen, who believes no such thing—perhaps because he is an atheist, or because he inclines to other gods—also has a veto over the contract. His consent too must be secured, and the law must be such that he could see reason to accept it. God's commandment is not a reason for him as it is for me, and therefore cannot be the ultimate ground of the law's legitimacy. The law must be grounded in considerations that provide a reason for everyone, regardless of religious beliefs.

Hobbes took the view that self-interest was the clue to rational choice, in this as in every other sphere, and that the social contract would be binding just so long as it was in the interest of each citizen to subscribe to it. Since life in a state of nature is "solitary, poor, nasty, brutish and short," all of us have a reason to put ourselves under the protection of a sovereign power, and everything necessary to the exercise of that power will be rationally acceptable to the subject. Religion, ideals, even moral principles play little or no part in the reasoning of Hobbes's subject—at least when it comes to the foundations of political obligation. The be-all and end-all of politics is rational self-interest, and it is this which establishes both the legitimacy and the limits of a secular rule of law.

Later contractarian philosophers differ from Hobbes in their theory of rational choice, and in the nature of the contract that they derive from it. But they tend to share

Hobbes's view that the social contract must be acceptable to all rational beings, and can therefore make no reference to matters over which there might be reasonable disagreement—religion being the first and most important of these. In its latest version, that articulated by John Rawls, the social contract theory goes a step further, removing all reference not merely to religion, but to the individual "conception of the good" which might distinguish one group of citizens from their neighbors.[5]

Rawls's aim is not to give grounds for political obligation, but to develop a theory of distributive justice. Moreover, his social contract is a highly artificial construction, existing (at least in its original version) as a hypothetical thought-experiment, against which moral intuitions can be measured and adjusted, and corresponding to no actual or implied agreement between citizens in a modern body politic. Nevertheless, it exemplifies the project initiated by the early contractarians—the project of removing from the legal order all reference to the sources of division and conflict between human groups, so as to create a society in which no question can arise that does not have a solution acceptable to everyone.

If religion, culture, sex, race, and even "conceptions of the good" have all been relegated to the private sphere, and set outside the scope of jurisdiction, then the resulting public law will be an effective instrument for the government of a multicultural society, forbidding citizens to make exceptions in favor of their preferred group, sex, culture, faith, or lifestyle. And while one may reasonably wonder at the miraculous correspondence between the "just society" as it emerges from Rawls's thought-experiment and the received ideas of liberal New York, this simply reinforces the status of the theory as the theology of a post-religious society. Rawls has taken to the limit—or rather, to one of its limits—the Western idea of a purely political order, in which all bonds of membership are contained within the abstract rights and duties of the citizen.

Like Hobbes, Rousseau, and Kant, Rawls relies on principles the validity of which he believes to be universal, and therefore acceptable to all people, whatever their history and condition. However, human societies are not composed of all people everywhere, and are indeed by their nature exclusive, establishing privileges and benefits that are offered only to the insider and cannot be freely bestowed on all comers without sacrificing the trust on which social harmony depends. The social contract begins from a thought-experiment, in which a group of people gather together to decide on their common future. But if they are in a position to decide on their common future, it is because they already have one: because they recognize their mutual togetherness and reciprocal dependence, which makes it incumbent upon them to settle how they might be governed under a common jurisdiction in a common territory. In short, the social contract requires a relation of membership, and one, moreover, that makes it plausible for the individual members to conceive the relation between them in contractual terms. Theorists of the social contract write as though it presupposes only the first-person singular of free rational choice. In fact it presupposes a first-person plural, in which the burdens of belonging have already been assumed.

Even in the American case, in which a decision was made to adopt a constitution and make a jurisdiction *ab initio*, it is nevertheless true that a first-person plural was involved in the very making. This is confessed to in the document itself. "We, the people . . ." Which people? Why, *us*; we who *already belong*, whose historic tie is now to be transcribed into law. We can make sense of the social contract only on the assumption of some such precontractual "we." For who is to be included in the contract? And why? And what do we do with the one who opts out? The obvious answer is that the founders of the new social order already belong together: they have already imagined themselves as a community, through the long process of social interaction that enables people to determine who should participate in their future and who should not.

Furthermore, the social contract makes sense only if future generations are included in it. The purpose is to establish an enduring society. At once, therefore, there arises that web of non-contractual obligations that links parents to children and children to parents and that ensures, willy-nilly, that within a generation the society will be encumbered by non-voting members, dead and unborn, who will rely on something other than a mere contract between the living if their rights are to be respected and their love deserved. Even when there arises, as in America, an idea of "elective nationality," so that newcomers may choose to belong, *what* is chosen is precisely not a contract but a bond of membership, whose obligations and privileges transcend anything that could be contained in a defeasible agreement.

There cannot be a society without this experience of membership. For it is this that enables me to regard the interests and needs of strangers as my concern; that enables me to recognize the authority of decisions and laws that I must obey, even though they are not directly in my interest; that gives me a criterion to distinguish those who are entitled to the benefit of the sacrifices that my membership calls from me, from those who are interloping. Take away the experience of membership and the ground of the social contract disappears: social obligations become temporary, troubled, and defeasible, and the idea that one might be called upon to lay down one's life for a collection of strangers begins to border on the absurd. Moreover, without the experience of membership, the dead will be disenfranchised, and the unborn, of whom the dead are the metaphysical guardians, will be deprived of their inheritance. The mere "contract between the living" is a contract to squander the earth's resources for the benefit of its temporary residents. And critics of Western societies do not hesitate to point out that that is exactly what is happening, as the contractual vision of society gains ground over the experience of membership that made it possible.

We are rational beings and have an inherent need to look for rational foundations for our institutions and laws—a need to which the various theories of the social contract answer. But we are also religious beings, with a need to submit to divine imperatives and to find comfort in the community of our fellow believers. And we are social beings, who live within boundaries dividing "mine" and "thine," and who join together to protect our common territory. As for the "conceptions of the good" which Rawls wishes to remake as private ideals, for the mass of mankind these reflect the desire for membership in a world larger, more meaningful, and more consoling than the realm of individual choice. A "conception of the good" will, in the normal case, be rooted in religious beliefs, rituals, customs, and primary loyalties. Few people with a genuine conception of the good believe it to be a private idiosyncrasy of their own that can and should be set aside in all matters of public decision-making. On the contrary, for most people a conception of the good is a necessary starting point for the building of a true society, and the knowledge that they live among people with different conceptions of the good is disturbing, alienating, and in the last analysis destructive.

Conceptions of the good console us because they come wrapped in certainty, rescued from the arbitrariness of choice, and pointing us with confident commands along the path of our salvation. The liberal thought-experiment is in fact the attenuated reflection of a particular kind of membership, and it is one that simply lacks credibility in societies where the political idea of membership has failed to replace the warm demands of religion. It is not possible for a Muslim to believe that the conception of the good that is so clearly specified in all the intricate laws and maxims of the Koran is to be excluded from the social contract. On the contrary, in Muslim eyes this conception, and this alone, gives legitimacy to the political order: a thought which has the disturbing corollary that the political order is almost everywhere illegitimate, and nowhere more so than in the states where Islam is the official faith.

MEMBERSHIP

People become conscious of their identity, and of the distinction between those who share it and those who do not, in many ways. Language, kinship, religion, and territory are all important, and all have fed into the various national and transnational ideologies that have animated modern politics. Political organization presupposes membership; but it also affects it, and many of the artificial states of the modern world have attempted to shape a "body politic" that will correspond to their borders and their laws through the invention of a "nation" of which they are the legal and political guardians. This process can be witnessed in the new states of Africa and Asia, formed from disintegrating empires. It can also be witnessed in the Middle East. But beneath the artificial divisions drawn on the map lie other and more visceral differences—differences of tribe, sect, language, loyalty, and lifestyle—which constantly threaten the web of laws and powers and boundaries that have been laid across them. When these visceral differences subvert or extinguish the secular law, cancel the rights of citizenship, and set group against group within the community, a country ceases to be part of the West and joins the rest—as is happening now in Zimbabwe.

To put the point in another way: Western civilization is composed of communities held together by a political process, and by the rights and duties of the citizen as defined by that process. Paradoxically, it is the existence of this political process that enables us to live without politics. Having consigned the business of government to defined offices, occupied successively by people who are the servants and not the masters of those who elected them, we can devote ourselves to what really matters—to the private interests, personal loves, and social customs in which we find our satisfaction. Politics, in other words, makes it possible to separate society from the state, so removing politics from our private lives. Where there is no political process, this separation does not occur. In the totalitarian state or the military dictatorship everything is political precisely because nothing is. Where there is no political process everything that happens is of interest to those in power, since it poses a potential threat to them. In Saddam's Iraq, as in Soviet Russia, social life is carried on furtively, under the vigilant eyes of a secret police force that can never be certain that it has discovered the real conspiracy that may one day destroy it.

Totalitarian states and military dictatorships are abnormalities. But so too, judged from the historical perspective, are states founded on the Western model. The political process is an *achievement*—one that might not have occurred and has not occurred in those parts of the world where Roman law and Christian doctrine have left no mark. Even today most communities are held together in other ways—by tribal sentiment, by religion, or by force.

The tribe is often described as "natural," meaning that it arises spontaneously and is never the result of a decision—certainly not of a political decision. Members of a tribe are joined by marriage and kinship, and the first-person plural is coextensive with the sense of kin (which may be amplified by the imagination to include all neighbors and familiars). Tribes can grow and take on a quasi-political structure, as their members move to foreign parts or lose touch with their ancestral community. Moreover, the majority of members of the tribe are either dead or unborn, and yet just as much members as those who are alive. This is what relations of kinship mean: you and I are descended from a common source, and owe our membership to the fact that our common ancestor is also a member. All tribal ceremonies in which membership is at stake—marriages, funerals, births, initiations—are also attended by the dead, who in turn are the guardians of those unborn. And the consolation of tribal membership resides partly in this union with absent generations, through which the fear of death is allayed and the individual granted the supreme endorsement of existing as a limb of the eternal organism.

Communities bound by religion—or "creed communities," to use Spengler's term[6]—grow naturally from the tribe, just as religion grows naturally from kinship. Through ceremonies of membership, in which the dead bear witness to our need of them, the gods enter the world. Every invocation of the dead is a transition to the supernatural; and whatever it is that people worship is located in the supernatural sphere: which is not to say that it is wholly outside nature or in any way inaccessible. On the contrary, the gods of the tribesman are as real and near to him as the spirits of his ancestors, and may be carried around in tangible form, like the household gods of the Romans. But that too is a sign of their supernatural character. For only what is supernatural can be *identical* with its own representation, as the god is identical with the idol, which exists nevertheless in a hundred replicas, each endowed with the same supernatural power.

The creed community is, however, distinct from the tribe. For here the criterion of membership has ceased to be kinship and has instead become worship and obedience. Those who worship my gods, and accept the same divine prescriptions, are joined to me by this, even though we are strangers. Moreover, creed communities, like tribes, extend their claims beyond the living. The dead acquire the privileges of the worshipper through the latter's prayers. But the dead are present in these new ceremonies on very different terms. They no longer have the authority of tribal ancestors; rather, they are subjects of the same divine overlord, undergoing their reward or punishment in conditions of greater proximity to the ruling power. They throng together in the great unknown, just as we will, released from every earthly tie and united by faith.

Creed communities can expand beyond the kinship relation most easily when they enjoy a sacred text, in which the truths about the divine order are set down for all time. The existence of such a text sanctifies the language in which it is written: the language is lifted out of time and change to become immemorial, like the voice of God. Hence, true creed communities resist not only changes to the ceremonies (which define the experience of membership), but also changes to the sacred text and to the language used in recording it. By this means Hebrew, Arabic, Latin, and the English of King James I have been lifted out of history and immortalized. Membership in the creed community may often require an apprenticeship in the sacred language: certainly no priest or mullah can be allowed to ignore it.[7] But the creed community inevitably grants privileges to the native speakers of that language, and endows them with a weapon that permits them to rule the world (or at least the only bit of the world that matters—the world of the faithful). The neighboring occurrence of two of the sacred languages—Arabic and Hebrew—as spoken languages in today's Middle East is of enormous socio-political importance. Although Hebrew has been strenuously revived in order to become a modern vernacular, and although spoken Arabic everywhere differs from the classical archetype, both languages resound with a message of religious membership. The fact that the languages are close cousins serves to fuel the conflict between those who speak them. For it is the one who is near to me, not the one who is far away and unrelated, who poses the greatest threat to my spiritual territory.

The initial harmony between tribal and credal criteria of membership may give way to conflict, as the rival forces of family love and religious obedience exert themselves over small communities. This conflict has been one of the motors of Islamic history, and can be witnessed all over the Middle East, where local creed communities have grown out of the monotheistic religions and shaped themselves according to a tribal experience of membership. There is at least one such community—the Druze—in which a credal idea of membership has come to depend on a tribal criterion. Each child of a Druze is held to be a member of the sect solely by virtue of his or her birth, and each new member of the sect is believed to inherit the soul of a Druze that died. The community can neither grow nor dwindle, but is an eternal communion of the unborn and the dead, each member of which is simultaneously in both conditions, while also being alive!

For a long time Europe existed as a kind of creed community—but one in which sovereignty had crystallized in the hands of individual families, whose claims were either endorsed by the Pope or asserted against him. But Christianity was a creed community with a difference. From its beginning in the Roman Empire it internalized some of the ideas of imperial government; in particular, it adopted and immortalized the greatest of all Roman achievements, which was the universal system of law as a means for the resolution of conflicts and the administration of distant provinces. Although Islam has its law, it is explicitly a holy law, laying down the path to salvation, and dealing with all the minute particulars—from the times of prayer to the rituals of personal hygiene—through which a person makes and unmakes his relationship with God. Moreover, this law derives its authority exclusively from the past, either from the word of God as recorded in the Koran or from the exemplary acts of the Prophet, as related in the Sunna. Jurisprudence is limited to tracing a decision back to those authoritative sources, or to some hadith of the Prophet that will fill the lacuna. The four orthodox schools (*madhahib*) of jurisprudence that emerged from the great period of Islamic civilization admitted the possibility of independent judgment or *ijtihad* (literally "effort," from the root *jahada,* "to strive," from which is derived also *jihad*, the "struggle on behalf of the faith"). But *ijtihad* must be based on the four roots or pillars of Islam—the Koran, the Sunna, *qiyas* ("analogy") and *ijma'* ("consensus")—and could not be used to introduce secular ideas of authority. Besides, it has long been accepted among Muslims that "the gate of *ijtihad* is closed," meaning that the divine law, the *shari'a*, can no longer be adjusted or added to, but merely studied for the meaning that it already contains.

The Roman law by contrast was secular, unconcerned with the individual's religious well-being. It was an instrument for governing people regardless of their credal differences; and its decisions were not validated by tracing them to some sacred source, but by autonomous principles of judicial reasoning and an explicit statement of the law. The law itself could change in response to changing circumstances; and its validity derived purely from the fact that it was commanded by the sovereign power and enforced against every subject.

That conception of law is perhaps the most important force in the emergence of European forms of sovereignty. It ensured the development of law as an entity independent of the sovereign's command, and the maintenance of a kind of universal jurisdiction through the courts of canon law. At the same time, each sovereign, through his own courts, was able to qualify and narrow the universal law so that it adapted itself to his territorial claims. Thus there arose the idea of kingdoms, not as local power centers, but as territorial jurisdictions the monarchs of which were constrained by the law and also appointed by it.[8] Often the law was, as in England, the creation of judges: and the common law principles (including those of equity) have ensured that, wherever the English law has prevailed, it is law and not the executive power that has the last word in any conflict between them.

Under the European experience of the sovereign state, therefore, territorial jurisdiction has had at least as much importance as language and religion in shaping people's attachments. Following the Reformation, three distinct conceptions of membership exerted their forces over the European imagination. First, religion, particularly those fine differences of doctrine and practice that distinguished Catholic from Protestant and sect from sect. (Fine differences are always more important in determining membership than large differences, precisely because they permit comparisons. The person whose religion differs from mine by a tiny article, or a barely perceivable gesture, is not a believer in other gods, but a blasphemer against my gods. Unlike the person with other deities, he is automatically an object of hostility, since he threatens the faith from a point within its spiritual territory.) Second, language, particularly the languages that had attained sanctity through some authoritative translation of the sacred texts (English and German, for instance), and that had been dispersed by the art of printing. And third, the gravitational force of territorial jurisdictions, under which contracts could be enforced, disputes settled, marriages and institutions legalized, with uniform effect over a continuous territory. In the course of time it was this last conception of membership that was to shape the modern world by laying the foundations for secular government, in which neither religion nor tribe nor dynasty would be the arbiter of collective choice, but in which all such factors would be subservient to the political process.

When law is defined over territory, so as to apply to everyone residing there, and when the source of its authority is the sovereign power, the reality of law, as a human artifact, rather than a divine command, becomes apparent. The law is detached from the demands of religion and reconstrued as an abstract system of rights and duties. It begins to show a preference for contract over status, and for definable interests over inarticulate allegiances.[9] In short, it becomes a great reformer of membership, coaxing it in a contractual direction. It makes our ties judiciable and therefore articulate; and in doing so it loosens them.

At the same time we must not think of territorial jurisdiction as a merely conventional arrangement, a kind of ongoing and severable agreement of the kind distilled in the social contract theory. It involves, in the normal case, a genuine "we" of membership: not as visceral as that of kinship; nor as uplifting as that of worship; and not as inescapable as those of language and kin; but a "we" all the same. For a jurisdiction gains its validity either from an immemorial past or from a fictitious contract between people who already *belong together*. In the English case, law comes with the authority of long usage; ancestors speak as clearly through it as they speak through the King James Bible; and the fact that English law is common law, arising from the particular decisions made in concrete cases and not through the impositions of a sovereign, gives to it an added authority as the "law of the land." Around this particular territorial jurisdiction, therefore, there has arisen a remarkable and in many ways unique form of membership, in which belonging is defined neither by language nor by religion nor even by sovereignty, but by the felt recognition of a particular territory as home: the safe, law-governed, and protected place that is "ours." As I have tried to show elsewhere,[10] this sense translates itself into a vision of the enchanted landscape. This vision did not come into being with the Lakeland poets, but has dominated English patriotism at least since Shakespeare's day, and, indeed, owes much of its power to thoughts and images articulated by Shakespeare. From this vision of the enchanted homeland arose the loyalty, the bravado, and also the "conception of the good" that built an empire.

Territorial jurisdictions sit uneasily upon credal communities, which tend to recognize the validity of no law other than the divine commands that shape their identity. This fact has been of great importance in the history of Islam, and also in the emergence of sovereign states in the Middle East and North Africa. For the true Muslim, no law is validated merely by deriving it from the customary law or sovereign edicts that establish a territorial jurisdiction. Laws can warrant our obedience only if they are divinely sanctioned; this means that their validity is established only if they can be derived from the *shari'a*—the revealed will of God. This conception of law has an immediate intelligibility in a society consisting purely of Muslims, members of a single sect, with an acknowledged tribal chieftain or ruling dynasty. But it is ill adapted to a society where rival confessions compete for a share in the collective assets, and where territorial boundaries between the communities are weak or non-existent. The Ottoman solution—the *millet* system—is worth considering, since it still survives, in altered form, in Lebanon, and provides an illustration of some of the problems that I shall be addressing in this book.

The Turkish term *millet* (which now has the meaning of "nation") derives from Arabic *millah*, meaning a creed community or sect. The Ottoman Empire included Christians and Muslims of almost every obedience, together with Jews, Druze, and Alawites (the latter two being sects that grew out of Islam but ought now to be regarded as indigenous forms of post-Islamic religion). Each subject of the Ottoman Empire belonged to, or was allocated to, a *millet*, defined primarily by religious custom and confession. The *millets* (*milletler* in Turkish) were represented separately before the Sultan's throne, and rivalry between them was settled by adjudication from the Sublime Porte—in that sense there was an overarching territorial jurisdiction. However, the authority of this jurisdiction depended upon the dominant *millet* of Sunni Muslims and on the *shari'a* as interpreted by the Mufti. When, during the nineteenth century, the Ottoman authorities attempted to modernize the law, as an instrument for administering the entire territory of the Empire, the resulting code—the Majalla, as it is known—was explicitly derived from the *shari'a*: the first attempt, indeed, to codify Islamic law. The Majalla was preserved under the British protectorate of Palestine, and incorporated after independence by the State of Israel: a tribute to Islam that is not often remarked upon.

The Ottoman Empire was a territorial jurisdiction only in the sense that the dominant creed community asserted its overarching control over all local administration. In all matters relating to religious custom, marriage, family, and inheritance the *millets* were sovereign, and they dealt with conflicts by a system of appeals to the office of their respective religious leader—the Greek Catholic Patriarch in Antioch, for example, or the Greek Orthodox Patriarch in Constantinople. The ones who suffered most from the Sunni ascendancy were not the Christian minorities (although the Armenians were to pay a bitter price when the Empire finally began to disintegrate), but the Muslim sects judged to be heretical and therefore deprived of a religious leader and communal identity of their own—the Shi'ites being the principal example.

As the Empire declined, the rights and privileges of

the *millets* were continually set aside by a central power that welcomed sectarian conflict as the best guarantee of its own survival. Increasingly, therefore, sectarian loyalties came to prevail over obedience to the Porte, and when, in the wake of the First World War, obedience was cancelled, the subjects of the Empire found themselves with no other lord than that which religious custom or tribal affiliation had bestowed on them. At the same time the Western powers—France and Britain in particular—were staking out their rival imperial claims in the region and dividing up the Ottoman territory into countries that had little or no identity beyond that required by administrative convenience and geopolitical strategy. Even where regions had achieved a kind of autonomy under Ottoman sovereignty—notably Lebanon and Egypt—the claims of history and local loyalty were largely set aside in the interests of imperial gain.

It is easy to blame the subsequent instability of the Middle East on the ambitions of the Western powers. However, it is important to bear in mind that, in a region of creed communities, none of which enjoyed a territory of its own, there was no alternative to empire. Without some kind of territorial jurisdiction imposed from outside, the communities themselves would have been bereft of all methods, other than war, of resolving the disputes between them. The Sykes-Picot accords, agreed between two adventurous diplomats charged with securing a postwar settlement for the region, therefore divided the Ottoman territories into geographical states, and endeavored to attach to each of them a sovereign who would command the common loyalty of the communities who resided there, and a legal system that would underpin the institutions required by political "progress."

These legal systems, derived as a rule by importing ready-made codes from the West, were intended to further the development of the territories as "nation-states," governed according to constitutional principles familiar from the European rule of law.[11] Although they frequently paid lip service to the *shari'a*, these codes harmonized badly with the indigenous legal traditions, and required knowledge and expertise that were not locally available. Hence the temporary imperial administrations under puppet sovereigns (some of whom had no previous territorial connection with the countries over which they nominally ruled) did not make way for genuine political government, still less for democracy in the Western mold, even in those countries—such as Egypt—where there was considerable indigenous support for Constitutionalism, and established interests wedded to the idea of a secular state. For the most part the regimes installed by the European powers crumbled before feudal despotism, hereditary monarchy, or the peculiar combination of gangster terrorism and Leninist one-party rule imposed through the Ba'th party by Hafiz el-Asad in Syria and Saddam Hussein in Iraq. And in place of Western ideas of secular government came the kind of raging ideological politics, influenced equally by Marxism and Islamic millenarianism, that finally gained absolute power with the Islamic Revolution of Khomeini in Iran.[12]

The most telling exception was Lebanon, which had retained a kind of independence since classical times. Thanks to its mountainous hinterlands, Lebanon had been able to protect itself from enemies (including the Sultan), and to survive as a semi-autonomous emirate, offering refuge to the more adventurous tribes of Asia Minor and the Fertile Crescent. And thanks to its Mediterranean harbors, Lebanon had enjoyed a freedom and respect for law that are the natural concomitants of maritime trade. Its Christian (largely Maronite) community (probably a majority at the time when Lebanon became a French protectorate) had evolved a territorial claim, a European sense of secular jurisdiction, and a commitment to freedom of conscience made necessary by its many sects.

Bordered by a despotic Syria, occupied by armed refugees from Palestine, invaded by the Israeli and Syrian armies, and beset by a rebellious and growing Shi'ite underclass and an Iranian-backed Shi'ite militia intent on bringing chaos to the countryside, Lebanon was doomed to destruction. Nevertheless, its model constitution and laws, its "national pact" (which distributed the offices of state according to the confessions), and its democratic procedures under a French-style presidency so distinguished it, during its years of relative peace, from every other Arab state as to bear witness to the real and deep difference between a Christian and a Muslim political culture. Territorial jurisdiction takes natural root in the first, but not in the second, and the one remaining example of a Muslim country in which secular jurisdiction and democratic procedures survive—Turkey itself—is notable for the fact that religion is expressly banished from the law, from the offices of state, and from the public life of the country, and that the edict of banishment must be constantly remade by a vigilant and secularized army.

With hindsight it is difficult to see the destruction of the Ottoman Empire as anything other than a disaster—a disaster whose consequences threaten to match those of the Russian Revolution and the rise of Hitler. So it is described by David Fromkin, for example.[13] The tragic history of the post–World War I settlement, however, is less relevant to today's world than the enduring failure of the Middle Eastern states to acquire territorial legitimacy. In this they contrast starkly with the successor states of the Austrian Empire, where nationalist aspirations had preceded the breakup of the Empire by a century or more, and where loyalties were already shaping themselves in the nineteenth century according to territorial rather than religious or tribal ideals.

Thus in the Czech and Slovak Republics we witness, following the collapse of communism, the emergence of a fully secular conception of citizenship, based in national loyalty and territorial integrity. Formed by the same kind of administrative fiat that had divided up the Ottoman

Empire, the former Czechoslovakia went through all the crises that are now familiar in multi-ethnic states. First the German minority voted *en masse* for the Nazi idea of an enlarged German homeland, while Hitler offered the Slovaks independence as a Nazi protectorate. Then, following the post–World War II expulsion of the Germans, the reunited Czechoslovakia fell under the Soviet yoke. Within two years of the communist fall from power in 1989, however, the state had split into the Czech and Slovak Republics, without violence and with the retention of a large number of social, institutional, and economic ties. Nothing comparable can be witnessed in the Middle East, where, apart from Turkey and Iran, communities are not defined by language and territory but by religion, tribe, and dynasty. The Czech and Slovak Republics have effortlessly taken on the character of the European *Rechtstaat* precisely because their pre-political loyalties were already shaped by national, rather than religious, ideals.

It is true that there has been a concerted attempt, beginning with the Ottoman reforms of the nineteenth century, to introduce ideas of national rather than religious unity into the Middle East. The philosophy of "Arab nationalism" was designed to facilitate modern forms of government, with the territorially defined nation (*qawm*) replacing the Islamic *umma* as the focus of loyalty. The Arab nation was invented in order to provide a pre-political order suitable to the emerging sovereign states, and "arabism" (*'uruba*) became a nationalist ideology designed to repair the religious and sectarian divisions among the Arabic-speaking peoples. It is perhaps significant that Michel Aflaq, the most influential modern proponent of Arab nationalism and co-founder of the Ba'th Party, was not originally a Muslim but a Paris-educated Syrian of Greek Orthodox extraction, who used nationalist rhetoric in order to uphold the claims of a "Greater Syria" against Lebanon and Israel.[14] When Aflaq, in later life, converted to Islam, it was because he saw this as the logical consequence of his Arabist ideology, rather than the other way around.

In fact the whole idea of Arab nationalism verges on contradiction, being an attempt to shape a local, territorial loyalty from a language that had been spread around the Mediterranean on the wings of a militant religion, and to conscript the religious loyalty that echoes in that most enchanted of languages to a secular cause with which it is profoundly incompatible. The Egyptian case is instructive. The quasi-autonomous Egyptian khedivate under Mehmet Ali and his successors began the Europeanizing process that severed the country from the rest of the Ottoman Empire. British occupation excited local resistance, the most effective and committed of which was that of the Muslim Brotherhood. This was founded by Hassan al-Banna in 1928, initially as a religious charity offering support and comfort to the migrants who were crowding into the cities, but soon developing into a terrorist movement aimed at ridding Egypt of alien powers. Resistance to the foreigner, in other words, came into being as a *jihad* on behalf of Islam. When Nasser came to power in 1952 by a coup d'état staged by fellow army officers, so ousting the British client King Faruq, he wished to gain legitimacy for a secular government, and therefore preached the Arab nationalist cause. But he found himself in immediate conflict with the real pre-political loyalty of the Muslim majority. The Copts of Egypt, like the Maronites and Melkites of Lebanon, saw the benefits of a secular state and Western systems of law: such is the normal Christian response. Many of the Muslims did not.

Nasser moved quickly to suppress the Muslim Brotherhood, by means almost as brutal as those which President Hafiz el-Asad was later to use in Syria. Having taken a step in this Arab nationalist direction, Nasser found himself compelled by the logic of the case to declare a short-lived "United Arab Republic" of Egypt and Syria. If the Arabs really are a unified people, then they deserve and require a unified state. The immediate collapse of the UAR, however, made it clear that there was little more to Arab *political* unity than a shared antipathy to Israel. The real unity remains today what it was in the time of Muhammad: the unity of a creed community with a common language sanctified by a holy text. And the centuries of fragmentation into rival sects and tribes have ensured that this unity—the only unity that the people really believe in—is also an unrealizable fiction whose political enactment entails bloodshed, tyranny, and war.

Anwar Sadat, who succeeded Nasser as President of

Egypt, recognized that the secular republic that Nasser had tried to create was unsustainable. Although the Muslim Brotherhood remained a proscribed organization, Sadat emphasized his own Islamic credentials and made apparent concessions to the mullahs, while at the same time urging a kind of local Egyptian nationalism—*msriah*—as the true basis of his political legitimacy. His assassination at the hands of religious terrorists was an especially vivid illustration of the fact that the most potent pre-political ideology to have captured the hearts of modern Egyptians has remained that of the Muslim Brotherhood. And it is to the Muslim Brotherhood that the atrocities of September 11 should ultimately be traced.

THE CHRISTIAN LEGACY

The social contract, I have suggested, is a kind of theological abstraction from the experience of territorial jurisdiction. It is a representation in ideal form of a committee, a coming together of people in a single place, in order to agree to the terms of their common protection. But the contract makes sense of Western politics only because of the long history that endowed Western communities with a territorial rather than a religious loyalty. I have referred to the role of Roman law in preparing the way for this. And I have emphasized the Christian distinction between *regnum* and *sacerdotium* as instilling the ideal of secular government in a people who are nevertheless bound by a common creed. But the history of the Middle East reminds us of a far more important legacy of Christianity, which is the extolling of forgiveness as a moral virtue.

The Muslim faith, like the Christian, is defined through a prayer. But this prayer takes the form of a declaration: There is one God, and Muhammad is his Prophet. To which might be added: and you had better believe it. The Christian prayer is also a declaration of faith; but it includes the crucial words: "forgive us our trespasses, as we forgive them that trespass against us." In other words, the appeal to divine mercy—which prefaces every sura of the Koran with the beautiful words *bism illah il-rahman il-rahim*, "in the name of Allah, the Compassionate, the Merciful"—is made conditional, in the daily prayer of Christians, upon the habit of forgiving our enemies. The "imitation of Christ" is conceived in the same terms: not as a vanquishing of God's enemies, but as a self-sacrifice, a willing oblation, an acceptance—in a spirit of forgiveness—of the worst that human beings can do. Needless to say Christians have not always followed this ideal, the Crusades being but one example. But it is also characteristic of Christianity that its adherents should apologize for the Crusades, taking on themselves the burden of a guilt incurred by their fellow believers, and seeking forgiveness from those whom their faith has wronged. Christianity contains within itself that idea of a political solution which Aeschylus presents in the *Oresteia*:

a solution that steps out of the cycle of vengeance in order to seek peace through conciliation.

The philosopher and critic René Girard sees this transition as critical to the Christian revelation.[15] In the absence of a judicial process, Girard argues, societies are invaded by "mimetic desire," as rivals struggle to match each other's social and material acquisitions, so heightening antagonism and precipitating the cycle of vengeance. The traditional solution is to identify a victim, one marked by fate as "outside" the community and therefore not entitled to vengeance against it, who can be the target of the accumulated bloodlust, and who can bring the cycle of retribution to an end. Scapegoating is society's way of recreating "difference" and so restoring itself. By uniting against the scapegoat people are released from their rivalries and reconciled.

Most religions incorporate this cycle of violence into themselves, and so legitimize it as the will of God. The triumph of Christianity, in Girard's eyes, is to have broken free from the cycle entirely. In the Gospels the scapegoat achieves transcendence and divinity through an acceptance of his fate, through an attitude of serene detachment from the aggressors, and through a manifest awareness that, while the aggressors do not know what they are doing, he does. For the first time the aggression that is at the root of the sacrificial rite is understood and forgiven by the victim, who is able both to accept his sacrifice and to believe in his own innocence. By freely offering himself as scapegoat, therefore, Christ lifted humanity from the cycle of "mimetic desire" and "mimetic violence," and into the realm of conciliation.[16]

That theory is of course highly controversial. Nevertheless, even without going so far as Girard, one must recognize that the idea of forgiveness, symbolized in the Cross, distinguishes the Christian from the Muslim inheritance. There is no coherent reading of the Christian message that does not make forgiveness of enemies into a central item of the creed. Christ even commanded us, when assaulted, to turn the other cheek. Pacifists take this remark to mean that we should not defend ourselves, but overcome violence as Christ did, by example. But it is possible to accept the Christian doctrine and yet to stop short of pacifism. Christ suffered the most violent death, not in order to recommend defenselessness, but in order to redeem mankind. At the same time he bore witness to the fact that it was not through *him* that evil had entered the world. In enjoining us to turn the other cheek he was setting before us, as always, a personal ideal, not a political project. If I am attacked and turn the other cheek, then I exemplify the Christian virtue of meekness. If I am entrusted with a child who is attacked, and I then turn the *child's* other cheek, I make myself party to the violence.

That, surely, is how a Christian should understand the right of defense, and how it is understood by the medieval theories of the just war. The right of defense stems from your obligations to others. You are obliged to protect those whom destiny has placed under your care. A political leader who turns not his own cheek but ours makes himself party to the next attack. Too often this has happened. But by pursuing the attacker and bringing him, however violently, to justice, the politician serves the cause of peace, and also that of forgiveness, of which justice is the instrument.

The Christian injunction to forgive is therefore compatible with defensive warfare. But it is incompatible with terrorism, and inimical to those visceral antagonisms that lead one group into a war of extermination against another. To remove the violent core from human societies is no easy task, for the urge to violence is planted in us by evolution, and war is a fact of sociobiology. Nevertheless, the Christian experience gives grounds for hope. Added to the tradition of secular law and territorial sovereignty, Christianity leads to the idea of a political order established without reference to tribe or faith, in which even the most fundamental differences can be accommodated, provided only that the territorial jurisdiction is given absolute sovereignty over those who reside within its borders.

The social contract provides the theology of such a territorial jurisdiction. But it does not, of itself, make such a jurisdiction possible. The political order as we in the West know it requires not only territory, but the sharing of it, and the sense of belonging that makes sharing possible. This sense of belonging does not come all at once, or without conflict. A group of incoming refugees, bound by family ties and religious duties to an amorphous "elsewhere," does not have the sense of belonging that is shared by the native population. It can acquire that sense, but only by renouncing an identity that binds it to another time and another place. Meanwhile it must rely on that habit of forgiveness and conciliation that tells the Christian to see the Other not as a threat but as an invitation to sympathy.

The triumph of America is that it has been able to persuade wave after wave of immigrants to relinquish all competing attachments and to identify with this *country*, this *land*, this great *experiment in settlement*, and to join in its common defense. Many factors have contributed to this triumph: but the hitherto prevailing Christian culture must surely be counted as the most important. In the next chapter, therefore, I shall explore the pre-political loyalty of such a modern democratic state, and point to some of the ways in which that loyalty is being eroded.

CHAPTER 2

ENLIGHTENMENT, CITIZENSHIP, AND LOYALTY

IN HIS CELEBRATED PLAY *Nathan the Wise* (1779), Gotthold Ephraim Lessing set out to dramatize the Enlightenment vision of benign political order, in which religions would co-exist in mutual toleration, and law would issue from the common humanity of the religious communities that enjoyed its protection. Set in the Holy Land during the time of the Crusades, the play tells the story of a Jewish merchant and his adopted Christian daughter, of the fanatical Templar who seeks the daughter's hand in marriage, and of the Muslim prince Saladdin, who resolves the tensions between his warring subjects by adopting Nathan's vision of a non-sectarian God. Whether or not the real Salah ad-Din—noble and generous though he reputedly was—espoused the Enlightenment vision that Lessing defended may be doubted. In any case, this majestic plea for tolerance should be seen for what it is: an essentially Western product, born of the emerging territorial jurisdiction that caused people to define themselves not in terms of their faith but in terms of their citizenship. It is unlikely that such a work should have been conceived under any Islamic regime, or that it should be on the reading list of a modern mullah. Such plausibility as pertains to Lessing's drama depends entirely on the fact that the chief protagonists are monotheists, able to agree—tacitly, if not explicitly—that their distinct forms of worship are merely several avenues to a single God.

Interestingly, this shared monotheism was built into the Lebanese Constitution of 1926, which declares its regime of toleration in Article 9:

> There shall be absolute freedom of conscience. The state in rendering homage to the Most High shall respect all religions and sects (*madhahib*), and shall guarantee under its protection a free exercise of all religious rites, provided that public order is not disturbed. It shall also guarantee that the personal status and religious interests of the people, to whatever community (*millah*) they belong, shall be respected.

The assumption that the Most High is the common object of worship translates the policy of toleration into the religious sphere. Secularism becomes a kind of religious duty, as well as a foundation of the confessional state. But the relentless war against Lebanon conducted by other Middle Eastern states shows how fragile is the Enlightenment vision enshrined in its constitution when transported to a region in which religion is still the warm lifeblood of the people, and not a private homage to an abstract God.

Such an abstract God was familiar, however, to the thinkers of Lessing's century. Voltaire and the Encyclopedists, Hume, Smith, and the Scottish Enlightenment, the Kant of *Religion within the Limits of Reason Alone*—such thinkers and movements had collectively remade the God of Christianity as a creature of the head rather than the heart. God retreated from the world to the far reaches of infinite space, where only vertiginous thoughts could capture him. Daily life is of little concern to such a God, who demands no form of obedience except to the universal precepts of morality. To worship him is to bow in private towards the unknowable. Worship conceived in such a way offers no threat to the Enlightenment conception of a purely legal citizenship, established by a social contract and maintained by a secular power.

As God retreated from the world, people reached out for a rival source of membership, and national identity seemed to answer to the need. Although the French revolutionaries paid homage with their heads to the Citizen, the Constitution, and the Republic, their hearts were captured by the Nation, the *Patrie*, the People, defined in terms of a visceral membership that demanded one thing above everything else—namely, human sacrifice. The idea of the citizen seemed eminently rational, peaceful, and serene. But the Nation burst into the political arena as an explosive, irrational, and destructive force, comparable to the political renewals of the Islamic *umma* today.

It is, in my view, impossible to understand the French Revolution if one does not see it as primarily a religious phenomenon.[1] The inner compulsion was to dethrone the gods of the monarchical order, and to erect a new community in its place—but a community demanding sacrifice, devotion, and slaughter, establishing a right to obedience through the spilling of blood. The leading revolutionary St-Just could say, in 1794, that a republic "is constituted by the total destruction of that which is opposed to it," so abolishing at a stroke the century of political thinking that had finally come to fruition in revolutionary France. Membership, as St-Just's remark makes clear, means the establishment of a "we," and the easiest way to invent this "we" is through a fight to the death with "them." The French Revolution was prodigal of opponents—some of them real, as in the Vendée uprising, some of them imaginary, like the quasi-supernatural *émigrés*, crystallizing now in this person or club or gathering, now in that, and everywhere the object of the most violent suspicion and enmity. There is no need to dwell on the parallels with subsequent revolutionary movements and their demons: the *émigrés* were simply the first in a long line of victims—kulaks, Jews, the bourgeoisie—prepared as sacrificial offerings on behalf of a new form of social membership. It is from a deficit of membership that the urge to revolution arises, and when people are hungry for membership, collective violence issues as a matter of course.

The French Revolution sought to replace one religion with another: hence its fanaticism and exterminatory zeal. But the new religion of the nation was demonic, fraught with contradiction and self-hatred, with no power to survive. It quickly gave way to the Napoleonic project of empire, through which violence was externalized and a rule of law re-established at home. In place of the attempt to build a religious form of membership with the nation as the Supreme Being, there came the desire for a political form of membership, in which the nation was the precondition of citizenship rather than the object of worship. France emerged from Bonaparte's defeat as a territorial jurisdiction based in national identity, rather than in a religion or a crown. Though both religion and monarchy had been restored under Bonaparte's regime, in altered and republicanized versions, it was the *code napoléon* and its promise of equal citizenship that confirmed the new identity of France. France gained what America had effortlessly bestowed on itself thirty years earlier: a concept of citizenship within a sovereign state ruled by a secular law.

Gradually, throughout the nineteenth century, this concept was spread across Europe; but it was spread because of a growing recognition among the peoples of Europe that their social membership was a matter of language, custom, and place, rather than religion or monarchical obedience. And where monarchies retained their hold over the sentiments of the people, it was where they were identified with a place, a language, and a legal order, as in Britain, Holland, and Scandinavia.

Now there are a great many differences between the American, the British, and the European forms of national loyalty. But they are all associated with territorial concepts of sovereignty and law, and secular ideas of citizenship. Which of these comes first in the order of things—national loyalty or territorial jurisdiction—is a matter of dispute. There are many who follow Lord Acton in arguing that nations are invented by the states that require them—that the new experience of membership has the function of legitimizing the new kind of legal order, and that this in some way explains its existence.[2] Some think that this is especially true of those nations born from the disintegration of colonial administrations, in which it is necessary for the artificial boundaries to be attached to "imagined communities" that will engender a new experience of legitimacy. Such is the theory given by Benedict Anderson in a now widely acknowledged study.[3] But it is a theory that only partially explains the emergence of nationhood in the Czech lands, in Poland, or in Germany. In any case, it is not pertinent to my theme to linger over this disputed question.

The point that I wish to emphasize is that the emergence of the modern Western state, in which jurisdiction is defined over territory, supported by secular conceptions of legitimacy, and associated with the rights and duties of citizenship, has also coincided with the emergence of a special kind of pre-political loyalty, which is that of the nation, conceived as a community of neighbors sharing language, customs, territory, and a common interest in defense. The nation-state did not come about painlessly, nor did it dispense with the need for those visceral attachments which enable people to call on the sacrifices that make communities durable. Nevertheless it was, until recently, the normal form in which Enlightenment ideas of legitimate government presented themselves. It is through the idea of the nation, therefore, that we should understand the pre-political loyalty presupposed in the contractarian view of citizenship.

National loyalty does not rule out religious obedience. The nations of Europe began life as Christian communities, and the boundaries between them often mark out long-standing religious divides—usually between Catholic and Protestant, though in some places between Catholic and Orthodox, or even Greek Catholic and Roman Catholic. Nevertheless, once the national idea gains ascendancy, religion is gradually reshaped in terms of it— which is why we distinguish Greek from Russian Orthodox, for example, or the Anglican from the Scandinavian forms of Protestant Christianity. The English experience is particularly important, since it involved the wholesale subordination of the priesthood to the head of state, himself regarded as bound by a territorial law that preceded his accession and also confirmed it.

In America religion has been a vital force in building

the nation. The initial unity of faith among the Pilgrim Fathers rapidly disintegrated, however, and while religious worship remains an important feature of the American experience, freedom of conscience has been guaranteed from the beginning by the Bill of Rights. This does not mean that America is a secular nation, or that religion has no part to play in establishing the legitimacy of American institutions. It means, rather, that all the many religions of America are bound to acknowledge the authority of the territorial law, and that each renounces the right to intrude on the claims of the state. Furthermore, these religions come under pressure to divert their emotional currents into the common flow of patriotic sentiment: the God of the American sects speaks with an American accent.

The patriotism that upholds the nation-state may embellish itself with far-reaching and even metaphysical ideas, like the theories of race and culture that derive from Herder, Fichte, and the German romantics.[4] But it might just as easily rest content with a kind of mute sense of belonging—an inarticulate experience of neighborliness—founded in the recognition that this place where we live is ours. This is the patriotism of the village, of the rural community, and also of the city street, and it has been a vital force in the building of modern America. Indeed, in the last analysis, national identity, like territorial jurisdiction, is an outgrowth of the experience of a common home.

Of course, if people turn their backs on one another,

live behind closed doors in suburban isolation, then this sense of neighborliness dwindles. But it can also be restored through the "little platoons" described by Burke and recognized by Tocqueville as the true lifeblood of America.[5] By joining clubs and societies, by forming teams, troupes, and competitions, by acquiring sociable hobbies and outgoing modes of entertainment, people come to feel that they and their neighbors belong together, and this "belonging" has more importance, in times of emergency, than any private difference in matters of religion or family life. Indeed, freedom of association has an inherent tendency to generate territorial loyalties and so to displace religion from the public to the private realm.

Membership defined through place encourages people to see law as "the law of the land." This effect is amplified in the English and American case by the common law. Although common to the whole territory this law arose from local judgments and not from decrees issued by the sovereign, whose tenure was traditionally regarded as conditional on his undertaking to uphold and adhere to the law of the land. The vast body of this law was, and remains, unwritten, except in the form of reports and commentaries. It is known as "case law," since it derives from the judgments delivered in individual cases. But it is not invented case-by-case, by the judges appointed to decide them. Rather, it advances by a process of discovery, in which evils are identified and remedies proposed, guided by principles of judicial reasoning that have their root in natural justice.[6]

The common law has stood like a shield between the individual and the sovereign power; it has always enjoyed a higher authority than the decrees of politicians for the simple reason that it is by virtue of the common law that the politicians hold office. To some extent this role of the law as a shield was rendered explicit in the first ten amendments to the U.S. Constitution. But those amendments themselves make sense only through their judicial interpretation, and they can be seen as re-enacting from on high protections already granted from below by the territorial jurisdiction of England.

The American and English sense of being "at home" in the mother country is therefore amplified by the legal culture, whose rules are seen as procedures for those who share a common territory. If that territory contains people whose religion differs from mine, or whose way of life diverges from anything that I would envisage for myself and my family, and if nevertheless they live by the rules and obey the legal requirements of our common housekeeping, I am obliged to tolerate their customs. Indeed, in these circumstances, a culture of toleration emerges of its own accord, and that is why the nation-state, which to many who study only its degenerate and belligerent forms seems a threat to Enlightenment values, is really the best guarantee that we have of a regime of toleration. For it is the transcription into political and sovereign form of the experiences of territorial loyalty and territorial law.

National loyalty arises only under certain conditions, however, the most important of which is the presence of a common language. And it is threatened by too great an attachment to exclusive ways of life, to militant religions, and to customs that invade the public space and privatize it in the interests of this or that inwardly turned sectarian feeling. One of the great difficulties facing Western societies today is that of integrating immigrant communities into a form of life that perceives exclusion, militancy, and public displays of religious apartness as threats to the experience of membership. And the perception here is self-confirming. That which is perceived as a threat becomes a threat. Such is the nature of home.

CITIZENSHIP

Unlike the Greek *polis*, the modern state is a society of strangers, bound together less by mutual rivalry and affection than by a sense of journeying side-by-side on the sea of fate. Our lives are subject to massive interference from people whom we do not know; and if we accept this, it is partly because of the regular flow of benefits, but much more because we recognize the common obedience that binds stranger to stranger in a web of mutual support.

There can be a seemingly stable social order in which the virtues of citizenship are unlauded and more or less unknown. Traditional Muslim Arab societies are stiff with obligations: obligations to family, to friends, to tribe; obligations that crisscross and overlap through competing networks of kinship and hospitality. And over these obligations is laid the supreme mantle of a divine law, which must be obeyed not because of human choice but in spite of it. Yet in such societies the interests of strangers go comparatively disregarded, and the law proves incompetent to resolve conflicts between people who have never met, or who do not subscribe to the official or majority religion.[7] The state is usually identified with a creed or a dynasty, and political obligation becomes obligation of another kind—of piety, kinship, or military subordination. The holy city of Mecca is situated in a country that is unique in the modern world in being named after the family that controls it. And the existence of a "Sa'udi" Arabia does much to explain both the fragility of the region's politics, and the sense of legitimacy through which the various factions assert their claims to the holy territory.

It is by contrast with such societies that the core idea of citizenship should be understood. The good citizen recognizes obligations towards people who are not, and cannot be, known to him. The Greek *polis* contained few living strangers, and those who roamed freely about its streets were expressly denied the gift of citizenship. They were the metics—the *metoikoi*—whose home or *oikos* was officially elsewhere. But the *polis* was generous towards dead and unborn citizens, honoring the first in every public ceremony, and providing for the second in all its deliberative acts. And it was in the course of honoring the dead that Pericles delivered the great oration that first defined the virtues of the free citizen. We Athenians pride ourselves, Thucydides has Pericles say, in being "free and tolerant in our private lives, in public matters obedient to the law."[8]

A modern democracy is perforce a society of strangers. And the successful democracy is the one where strangers are expressly included in the web of obligation. Citizenship involves the disposition to recognize and act upon obligations to those whom we do not know. The comparative absence of this disposition from the Islamic countries in the Middle East has had catastrophic consequences, as attitudes shaped by religion and family ties try to adapt themselves to a world made by strangers. The clatter of industrial progress, the remorseless technological change, the constant uprooting, pillaging, and tearing down, the tireless glare of the media, the irresistible invasions by the state and its agents—all this amplifies the desire to seek refuge in family, tribe, or religion, and to divide the world into friends and foes. But these attitudes, however understandable, also invite the dictator to take charge. Citizenship enables strangers to stand side-by-side against authority and assert their common rights. It therefore provides a shield against oppression, and an echo to the dissenting voice. Without this recourse there is no outlet for opposition, except through a conspiracy to subvert the ruling power.

Western democracies did not create the virtue of citizenship; on the contrary, they grew from it. Nothing is more evident in the *Federalist* than the public spirit that it invokes, in opposition to factions, cabals, and private scheming. As Madison pointed out, democratic elections do not suffice to overcome faction, or to instill a true sense of public answerability into the hearts of those who are elected. Only in a republic—a system of representational offices filled by citizens held answerable to those who elected them—will true patriotism animate the workings of power.[9] The Constitution of the United States was successful largely because those who devised it sought to found a republic in which the obligation to strangers would find concrete embodiment in the institutions of the Union: a republic in which factions would have only social, rather than political, power. Democracy was adopted as a means to this goal; but it is a dangerous means, and depends upon maintaining the public spirit of the citizens if it is not to degenerate into a battleground for special interests. It is a characteristic error of the times in which we live to identify the virtue of citizenship with the democratic spirit, so encouraging the belief that the good citizen is simply the person who puts all questions to the vote. On the contrary, surely: the good citizen is the one who knows when voting is the *wrong* way to decide a question, as well as when voting is the right way. For he knows that his obligations to strangers may be violated when majority opinion alone decides their fate. That is part of what Tocqueville and Mill had in mind when warning us against the tyranny of the majority.[10] The crucial feature of a republican constitution is not democracy, but representation, and this in turn requires a territorial jurisdiction, along with the loyalties that feed it. These loyalties become durable through the three paramount virtues of the citizen: law-abidingness, sacrifice in war, and public spirit in peacetime.

To lay down your life for a friend is hard. To do so for a stranger harder still. Yet without the disposition to renounce life for the common good, a society of strangers cannot survive. It is in reflecting on this matter that we see the need to ally the idea of citizenship with a territorial loyalty. People lay down their lives for their gods and their families, since it is in the nature of gods and families to demand this. But they do not normally lay down their lives for strangers—perhaps only Christ has gone so far in self-abnegation. However, people have an instinct to defend their territory, and to regard it as sacred. This too can be the source of sacrifice, and it is from the love of the "fatherland" or "motherland" that the heroism of the citizen derives. This was already evident to the ancients, and Horace's "dulce et decorum est/ pro patria mori" captures the spirit of the citizen-soldier.

When considering why it is that Western civilization has spread so far and proved so durable, one should not ignore the merits of the citizen-soldier as a weapon. According to Victor Hanson,[11] the civic culture of the Western soldier produces an unmatched combination of group discipline and inventive decision-making. Faced with the vast slave armies of oriental despots, the disciplined phalanxes of free citizens will tend always to acquit themselves with glory, and the great landmark battles that extended or defended Western borders have been decided by the kind of courage, discipline, and self-sacrifice that stem from civic patriotism.

Public spirit is perhaps the most misunderstood of all the features of citizenship, and the one that has been most precious in Anglophone history. The public-spirited person gives time, energy, and resources for the benefit of others whom he does not know, and with a view to perpetuating the social order of which he is a beneficiary. He is the founder of schools, hospitals, and facilities for the use of those unborn. He is first on the scene of a disaster, and the one who will turn indignation on another's behalf into a campaign to rescue him. Public spirit has abounded in England and America, animated by the sense of the "homeland" as a place of charity, harmony, and goodwill.

The citizen, to put the point succinctly, shares his membership with people whom he does not know, and to whom he is bound in a common web of rights and duties. When St. Paul described the early church, he gave voice to a similar idea, saying that "we are members one of another." But he also implied that this membership might spread across the globe. Such universal membership is the aim of both the Christian and the Muslim religions, which derive their authority from a timeless and transcendental

God. But it is not the aim of citizenship. Citizens remain bound to a particular temporal community, and their law-abidingness is expressed in their obedience to the law of that community. It is this community that they defend in war, and which they build in peace through charitable works and public spirit. Of course, they have other and wider duties, and the Christian religion in particular makes a large and exacting demand on them. But the obligations of citizenship are determined by the historically given reality into which the citizen is born.

The community of strangers cannot really be understood without reference to other generations. It is an *inherited* community. The true citizen inevitably includes among the strangers to whom he is obligated both ancestors and offspring. In any crisis this becomes immediately clear. A threat of war or invasion, an economic collapse, or some unprecedented damage to the social fabric all turn our attention to the historical community. It is *we* who now must fight, must put our backs to the wheel, must mend our ways; and this "we" includes absent generations, as well as those now living. It would be easy for the English to renounce their loyalty to the crown, to forget their ancestors, to throw away the culture and inheritance of their country, and to become "citizens of Europe," were it not for the fact that, in doing so, they would lose the roots of their social membership. The debate over Europe makes abundantly clear that good citizens remain attached to and dependent upon an ancestral "we." In the last analysis, the modern citizen belongs to a nation, and the nation commands our loyalty not just because of what it is, but because of what it has been and will be through its own reproductive powers.[12]

When Burke wrote of society as a partnership between the living, the unborn, and the dead, this was what he had in mind.[13] The partnership is evident in those small and custom-bound societies which define themselves through kinship. But it is equally evident in a society based on citizenship, like the modern United States, which derives from recent and remembered patterns of immigration. The assumption has been that I am committed to the living strangers who surround me because they are bound in the same web of connections as I. Our people have stood side-by-side in this territory, and built the social and cultural inheritance that we both enjoy. We must protect and enhance it, in order that our children shall stand together in their turn. The fact that myths and historical distortions are necessary in order to sustain this assumption is neither here nor there. That is how citizenship is, and must be, understood.

The commitment to absent generations can be viewed in another way. In all its manifestations, citizenship involves rising above the present moment and adopting the long-term view. Law-abidingness involves the renunciation of appetite for the sake of the territorial law. The law stands firm until judgments amend it. It is an overarching mantle, stretched across the common territory, and under it a society conducts and resolves its day-to-day disputes and conflicts. Law-abiding people automatically look on the society to which they belong as an enduring thing, reaching before and after their narrow life spans, and demanding a renunciation of appetite precisely so that things may endure. They abide by the law because the law abides.

Citizens who risk their lives for strangers are also disposed to take the long-term view. It is very difficult to contemplate the sacrifice of your life without believing in the durability of the thing for which you die. The patriot who dies in defense of territory and the people who have settled there is not laying down his life for some temporary arrangement, but defending what is or aims to be permanent. One of the difficulties now facing Western societies is that this species of virtue is rapidly disappearing. The intrusion of the media into the battlefield has had a shattering effect on the perception of war. And the declining birthrate and increasing longevity of the population have made Western societies ever more reluctant to risk in combat their dwindling supply of sons.

Like patriotic sacrifice, public spirit and charitable giving make little sense without the long-term perspective. Their entire purpose, in the minds of those who engage in them, is to make a permanent difference to the world—to improve the lot of others and of the community in such a way that the public realm is enriched and guarded against extinction. Hence the importance to these activities of the *endowment*. Public spirit and charitable giving are institution-building forces, through which private individuals realize their nature by creating durable forms of social life.

The three virtues that sustain the gift of citizenship have their equivalents in Muslim societies. The Muslim must abide by the *shari'a*; he must be prepared to sacrifice himself in *jihad*; and he must pay a tenth of his goods to the *zakat*. But these are duties owed to God, not to strangers, and the meticulous fulfillment of them may sometimes heal society, and sometimes blow it apart.

NATIONHOOD

Citizenship, as I have defined it, is the goal and aspiration of Western political systems, and the criterion of their legitimacy. Citizens enjoy rights—both the "human rights" or "natural rights" that are the pre-condition of their consent to be governed, and the right of participation in the political process. They are also bound by duties to their fellow citizens, and these duties spring from a peculiar experience of membership. Citizens are first and foremost members of a society of strangers, committed to the defense of their common territory and to the maintenance of the law that applies there. Citizenship therefore depends on pre-political loyalties of a territorial kind—loyalties rooted in a sense of the common home and of the transgenerational society that resides there. In short, citizenship as we know it depends on the nation, defined as a self-renewing organism clothed in the mantle of a law-governed state.

Ever since Kant, liberal thinkers have dreamed of another kind of citizenship—world citizenship, in which national loyalties would be extinguished in an all-embracing legal order free from the causes of belligerence (competition for territory being chief among them), and in which the warm relations of membership would be replaced by a cool adherence to a scheme of abstract duties and rights. However, every attempt to replace national loyalty with some internationalist ideal threatens the historical balance of power and the local forms of equilibrium that depend on it. Of course, the nation-state is not the only possible form of pre-political membership. But the alternatives—tribes, creed communities, or customary communities united by an imperial power—are no longer available to us, and in any case are hostile, on the whole, to democratic politics. Nationhood is the best that we can offer by way of a pre-political loyalty that delivers territorial jurisdiction and individual citizenship as its natural political expressions.

However, nations must be renewed. The strength of the national idea is that it can be renewed from so many sources: from youth movements, from education, from marriage and the family, and from a patriotic culture expressed in word and song and film. The weakness of the national idea is that all those ways of renewal are tentative when not endorsed and protected by a single overarching religion. When the news came of the September 11 attacks, many immigrant communities in France, Germany, and Britain took to the streets in rejoicing. It became suddenly apparent—what the liberal establishment has been trying for a decade or more to conceal—that the loyalties on which the European *Rechtstaat* are founded are not automatically shared by those who come from elsewhere to enjoy their protection.

Consider the mad mullah of Finsbury Park, Abu Hamza al-Masri, now wanted in Yemen on charges of conspiracy to murder. Hamza al-Masri came to Britain seeking asylum, and in order to enjoy the freedoms in defense of which British troops are currently risking their lives. Taking advantage of a freedom of speech nowhere available in the Islamic world, al-Masri used his Friday sermons to incite young men to violence and holy war, and named Britain, among other places, as a legitimate target. The Yemeni government alleges, on very good grounds, that he has sent a group of British Muslims to Yemen in order to bomb the British Embassy there and at the same time to kidnap and murder British tourists.

Many people, observing such cases, ask why Western governments permit representatives of minorities to express hatred and belligerence of a kind that would lead to an old-fashioned Englishman or Frenchman being put behind bars. The answer is simple: a loss of national identity, and of the old experience of membership that goes with it. The official view in most Western countries is that we are multicultural societies, and that cultures should be allowed complete freedom to develop in our territory, regardless of whether they conform to the root standards of behavior that prevail here. As a result, the "multicultural" idea has become a form of apartheid. All criticism of minority cultures is censored out of public debate, and newcomers quickly conclude that it is possible to reside in a European state as an antagonist and still enjoy all the rights and privileges that are the reward of citizenship. This is the principal reason why efforts in Britain to recruit immigrant minorities to the police and armed forces—in other words, to the professions that symbolize our territorial jurisdiction and its claims on us—have met with such scant success.[14]

Those who express doubts about the "multicultural society" are not, as their opponents hasten to call them, racists. They are trying to remind people that we in the "West" enjoy a *single* political culture, with the nation-state as the object of a common loyalty, and a secular conception of law, which makes religion a concern of family and society, but not of the state. People who see all law, all social identity, and all loyalty as issuing from a religious source cannot really form part of this political culture, and will not recognize either the obligation to the state or the love of country on which it is founded. This does not mean that religion should be excluded entirely from the affairs of state, or that we should endorse the kind of fanatical expulsion of faith from public institutions that has recently been practiced in America. On the contrary: the liberal belief in the separation of state and civil society implies that religion may thrive in all social institutions in which the citizens wish it to thrive. Thus, for example, prayers can occur in school (which is not a political institution, but a social institution funded by the state) without violating the principle of secular government.

Nevertheless, even the most religious of ordinary Americans will recognize that the state itself should not be subject to religious control. And when it comes to questions of sovereignty and defense they acknowledge that the Constitution and the rule of law take precedence over all religious loyalties. America is a new country; few of its communities have been established there long enough to think that they have an absolute right of precedence, and the prevailing culture of enterprise, freedom, and the pursuit of success absorbs America's many diverse religions into a single cooperative venture. The first effect of the recent atrocities was to awaken Americans to the fact that their loyalties are not global and religious, but local and secular. The American people stand and fall together as a nation; and it is as a nation that they are hated by the extremists.

Hence, although the Americans are religious people, and include many Muslims among their number, the law to which they owe obedience is the law of the United States. This law makes no religious demands, binds all Americans equally to a place and its history, and safeguards a political heritage in which the freedom of the individual is the highest aim of government. It is the very success of America in founding a common loyalty without a shared religious faith that so incenses the Islamist extremists.

As in the American case, the rights and duties of the British citizen are defined without reference to the will of God. A British Muslim is as much bound by the duties of the citizen as a British Christian or a British atheist. It is no more acceptable for British Muslims to say that their religion absolves them from obedience to the territorial law than it is for any other group of British citizens. A spokesman for al-Muhajiroun ("Émigrés" or "Exiles," a group founded in Britain and with links to Osama bin Laden) recently warned that no British Muslim has any obligation to British law when it conflicts with the law of Allah, and that the British mujahideen in Afghanistan, waiting to fight there against what others would call "their country," must remain indifferent to any charge of treason.

And at one level the spokesman is right. Christians will agree that obedience to the secular law is impossible when that law conflicts with the law of God. But there is a great difference between the Christian and the Islamic interpretation of what this means. For the Christian the law of God coincides with the moral precepts laid down in the Ten Commandments, which were reduced by Christ to just two—namely, to love God entirely and to love your neighbor as yourself. These commandments do not replace the secular law but *constrain* it. They set limits to what the sovereign can command: but so long as the sovereign does not transgress those limits, the secular law retains absolute authority over the citizen.

Islamic jurisprudence does not recognize secular, still less territorial, jurisdiction as a genuine source of law. It proposes a universal law that is the single path (*shariʻ*) to salvation. And the *shariʻa* is not understood as setting limits to what can be commanded, but rather as a fully comprehensive system of commands—which can serve a military just as well as a civilian function. Nor does Islam recognize the state as an independent object of loyalty. Obedience is owed first to God, and then, below him, to those situated at greater or lesser remove in the web of personal obligations. Nor is there any trace in Islamic law of the secular conception of government that Christianity inherited (via St. Paul) from Roman law.

Religious toleration is the norm in Western societies precisely because they are founded on a territorial jurisdiction that regards sovereignty rather than divinity as the source of law. Once we begin to think like al-Muhajiroun, that conception of political loyalty will be at an end, and each religious, ethnic, or nationalistic group within our borders will have complete license to take up arms against the heretic and the unbeliever. To insist that British Muslims owe their loyalty to the country of their citizenship is not to defy or oppress their legitimate religious aspirations. It is to uphold the way of life and the political culture that makes it possible for them, and for their fellow believers, to live in Britain in peace. If there are British Muslims who wish to defy this way of life and take up arms against the British state, then so be it. But the correct name for what they do is treason.

The case of al-Muhajiroun reminds us, however, of the root causes of the current crisis. Membership is not a luxury but a need. In simple societies this need is fulfilled by "rites of passage," ceremonies of initiation and transition whereby people acquire the full rights and duties of the community. These ceremonial transitions survive in modern societies, but in "privatized" form. Barmitzvahs, christenings, first communions, marriages, etc., are "family" affairs, not reaching out into the community of strangers but forming small intimate bubbles of consolation in the backwater of the suburban home. Young people still aspire to membership, through team and school. But the experience is intensely localized and often without the links to the nation and its symbols that, in the past, served to channel the social emotions towards a common pool of loyalty.

The ruling problem of Western societies today, then, is this: the experience of membership required by the Enlightenment idea of the citizen is dwindling, and a "culture of repudiation" is coming in its place. Young people gain nothing from this culture save bewilderment and the loss of any sense of identity. If they come from immigrant backgrounds that preserve the memory of a religious law, they will often enthusiastically revert to a religious experience of membership, and define themselves in opposition to the territorial jurisdiction by which they are ostensibly governed.

THE CULTURE OF REPUDIATION

The Enlightenment vision of our condition, transcribed into laws and institutions that guarantee the rights of the citizen, is one of the most noble of human dreams. But rights must be paid for by duties, and the call to duty is effective only in the context of a common loyalty. When loyalty erodes, the sense of duty erodes along with it. At the same time the erosion of duty is accompanied by no diminution in the call for rights. On the contrary, as people neglect their duties they assume, reasonably enough, that others are doing likewise. The result is a ubiquitous amplification in the demand for rights. The political process becomes a scramble to claim as much from the common resources as they will yield, and the jurisdiction is treated as a commercial venture, with litigation as the means to gain a competitive advantage over one's fellow citizen.[15]

At the same time, man cannot live by rights alone. My right is your duty, and in a culture of rights I am inevitably aware that I am presuming on the dutifulness of others and on their disposition to obey the law. However ruthlessly I pursue my own rights at your expense, I know that this is possible only because of our common loyalty and shared membership. This presumption of a common loyalty is felt as a moral burden, and as a religious, or quasi-religious, need. Unable to affirm the old forms of membership, people repudiate them instead, hoping that a newer and more acceptable kind of membership will arise from the ashes of denial.

The most important illustration of this phenomenon is the family. Religious societies generate families automatically as the by-product of faith. God, it seems, has a consuming interest in our sexual lives, and it is not difficult to understand why. For it has been evident at least since Durkheim's great treatise, *The Elementary Forms of the Religious Life,* that religions exist first and foremost because they offer membership, in a form that will dedicate people to the collective task of social reproduction. A religious community is better equipped to survive in any conflict, by virtue of the social cohesion, shared obedience, and dedication to the long-term view that all stem naturally from the discipline of faith. Religion also solemnizes marriages, dedicates parents to children, and binds generation to generation in a web of indestructible vows.

In a secular society, however, the family is without that all-important fund of moral and ideological support. It begins to seem less and less like a divinely sanctioned duty and more and more like a defeasible human choice. One mark of modern conservatism has been its iconization of the family as an object of intrinsic value. The family, no longer seen as the necessary by-product of faith, becomes an end in itself, the source, rather than the product, of communal values. We see this iconization of the family clearly in the first important theoretical works of modern conservatism—Hegel's *Philosophy of Right* and Burke's *Reflections on the French Revolution*—and in the remaking of the European monarchies in the nineteenth century as "Royal Families" whose rule was validated by their benign domesticity. And the emphasis on family values remains today as a forlorn cry of the conservative voice, summoning us away from our pleasures. As loyalties and pieties dwindle—with divorce, promiscuity, and a general evasiveness towards long-term commitment—there arises a new attitude towards the family: one not of skepticism but of repudiation. The family is denounced as a source of oppression, or as a patriarchal institution dedicated to the subordination of women.

Shortly after the family had been iconized by Hegel, it was satirized by Marx and Engels in *The Holy Family*. But the real intellectual war against the family is a product of the late twentieth century, and part of a great cultural shift from the affirmation to the repudiation of inherited values. Wilhelm Reich, R. D. Laing, Aaron Esterson, and radical psychotherapists of their persuasion see the family as a burden imposed by the past: a way in which parents encumber their offspring with an inheritance of defunct authority. Schizophrenia, in Laing's view, arises because the Self is made Other by the parental imposition of dysfunctional norms. Following the lead set by such thinkers, and by Michel Foucault in his "histories" of sexuality, madness and medicine, radical feminism has set out to deconstruct the family entirely, exposing it as an instrument of male domination, and advocating new kinds of "negotiated" union in its place.

There remains a section of society that is solidly committed to "family values," and to the division of roles that makes families durable. But this section of society does not have any real voice in the shaping of public opinion. The message of the media, the academy, and the opinion-forming elite is feminist, anti-patriarchal, and opposed to traditional sexual prohibitions such as those governing abortion, homosexuality, and sex outside marriage. More importantly, the culture of the elite has undergone a kind of "moral inversion," to use Michael Polanyi's idiom.[16] Permission turns to prohibition, as the advocacy of alternatives gives way to a war against the former orthodoxy. The family, far from enjoying the status of a legitimate alternative to the various "transgressive" postures lauded by the elite, is dismissed out of hand as a form of oppression.

An old structure of social membership has proved untenable; and by repudiating it we briefly enjoy a new form of membership as comrades-in-arms against the past. Membership, when offered in this way—fresh, rejuvenating, a bid to cleanse and liberate the world—is a covert appeal to the religious, rather than the political, experience of society. Feminism claims, like Marxism, to be a political movement; but it is in fact a movement against politics, just as Marxism has been. It seeks to replace or rearrange the core experience of social membership and therefore has the ambitions of a monotheistic faith, offering a feminist answer to every moral and social question, a feminist account of the human world, a feminist theory of the universe, and even a feminist reading of the Goddess. It drives the heretics and half-believers from its ranks with a zeal that is the other side of the inclusive warmth with which it welcomes the submissive and the orthodox. And it stands implacably opposed to the old order, in something like the way that Protestantism stood opposed to the Roman Catholic Church during the Renaissance.

At the same time, feminism—at least in its academic versions—sees itself as heir to the Enlightenment, continuing the impartial pursuit of truth to the point where it subverts the assumptions on which traditional society was founded. Like Marxism, feminism purports to show us the world without ideological masks or camouflage. Nevertheless, it too has an ideological purpose. Its repudiating zeal is not, as a rule, directed against Islam or the cultures of the East. It is directed against the West, and its message is "down with us."

Such is a general truth about political correctness, of which feminism is an obligatory component. While exhorting us to be as "inclusive" as we can, to discriminate neither in thought, word, nor deed against ethnic, sexual, or behavioral minorities, political correctness encourages the denigration of what is felt to be most especially *ours*. The director-general of the BBC recently condemned his organization and its programs as obnoxiously white and middle class. Academics sneer at the curriculum established by "Dead White European Males." A British race-relations charity has condemned the affirmation of a "British" national identity as racist. And so on. All such abusive utterances conform to the code of political correctness. For although they involve the deliberate condemnation of people on grounds of class, race, sex, or color, the purpose is not to include the Other but to condemn Ourselves. The gentle advocacy of inclusion masks the far-from-gentle desire to exclude the old excluder: in other words to repudiate the cultural inheritance that defines us as something distinct from the rest.

The "down with us" mentality is devoted to rooting out old and unsustainable loyalties. And when the old loyalties die, so does the old form of membership. Enlightenment, which seems to lead of its own accord to a culture of repudiation, thereby threatens Enlightenment. For it undermines the certainties on which citizenship is founded. This is what we are now witnessing in the intellectual life of the West.

In place of the Enlightenment emphasis on reason as the path to objective truth has come the "view from outside," in which our entire tradition of learning is put in question as a preliminary to its rejection. The old appeal to reason is seen merely as an appeal to Western values, which have made reason into a shibboleth, and thereby laid claim to an objectivity that no culture could possibly possess. For cultures offer membership, not truth, and can therefore make no exclusive claims on the one who sees them from a point of view outside their territory. Moreover, by claiming reason as its source, Western culture has (according to the fashionable "postmodernist" critique) concealed its ethnocentrism; it has dressed up Western ways of thinking as though they had universal force. Reason, therefore, is a lie, and by exposing the lie we reveal the oppression at the heart of Western civilization.

The dethroning of reason goes hand-in-hand with a hostility to the belief in objective truth. The authorities whose works are most often cited in debunking "Western culture" are all opponents of this belief. And, like the laws of logic, the belief in truth and rational argument is impossible to defend without at the same time presupposing it. A kind of intellectual impasse therefore confronts the defenders of the old curriculum and the discipline expressed in it, and they watch in silence as the new anti-authoritarian authorities colonize their patch.

Nietzsche is a favorite, since he made the point explicitly: "There are no truths," he wrote, "only interpretations." Now, either what Nietzsche said is true—in which case it is not true, since there are no truths—or it is false. But it is only from the standpoint of the Enlightenment that this response seems like a refutation. The new curriculum is in the business of marginalizing refutation, just as it marginalizes truth. This explains the appeal of those recent thinkers—Michel Foucault, Jacques Derrida, and Richard Rorty—who owe their intellectual eminence not to their arguments but to their role in giving authority to the rejection of authority, and to their absolute commitment to the impossibility of absolute commitments. In each of them you find the view that truth, objectivity, value, or meaning are chimerical, and that all we can have, and all we need to have, is the warm security of our own opinions.[17] Hence it is in vain to argue against the new authorities. No argument, however rational, can counter the massive "will to believe" that captures their normal readers. After all, a rational argument assumes precisely what they "put in question"—namely, the possibility of rational argument. Each of them owes his reputation to a kind of religious faith: faith in the relativity of all opinions, including this one. For this is the faith on which a new form of membership is founded—a first-person plural of denial.

In its own eyes the Enlightenment involved the celebration of universal values and a common human nature. The art of the Enlightenment ranged over other places, other times, and other cultures, in a heroic attempt to vindicate a vision of man as free and self-created. That vision inspired and was inspired by the old curriculum, and it has been the first concern of the postmodern university to put it in question. This explains the popularity of another relativist thinker—Edward Said, whose striking book *Orientalism* showed how to dismiss Enlightenment itself as a form of cultural imperialism.[18] The Orient appears in Western art and literature, Said argues, as something exotic, unreal, theatrical, and therefore unfounded. Far from being a generous acknowledgement of other cultures, the orientalist art of Enlightenment Europe (including Lessing's *Nathan the Wise*) is a screen behind which those cultures are concealed. The Orient might have been a genuine alternative to Western Enlightenment; instead it is remade as a decorative foil to the Western imperial project.

On this view the old Enlightenment curriculum is really monocultural, devoted to perpetuating the view of Western civilization as inherently superior to its rivals. It is also the product of Dead White European Males who have since lost their authority. And its assumption of a universal rational perspective, from the vantage point of which all humanity could be studied, is nothing better than a rationalization of its imperialist claims. By contrast, we who live in the amorphous and multicultural environment of the postmodern city must open our hearts and minds to all cultures, and be wedded to none. The inescapable result of this is relativism: the recognition that no culture has any special claim to our attention, and that no culture can be judged or dismissed from outside.

But once again there is a paradox. For those who advocate this multicultural approach are as a rule severely critical of Western culture. While exhorting us to judge other cultures on their own terms, Said is also asking us to judge Western culture from an external perspective—to set it against alternatives, and to judge it adversely as ethnocentric. In Said's case the paradox runs deep; for he has a profound knowledge of the art of music, and displays in his musicological writings precisely the humane and enlightened universalism that has made tonal music into the symbol of Western culture.

Furthermore, the criticisms offered of Western culture are really confirmations of its claim to favor. It is thanks to the Enlightenment, and its universalist morality, that racial and sexual equality have such a commonsense appeal to us. It is the Enlightenment conception of man that makes us demand so much of Western art and literature—more than we should ever demand of the art and literature of Java, Borneo, or China. It is the very attempt to embrace other cultures that makes Western art a hostage to Said's strictures—an attempt that has no parallel in the traditional art of Arabia, India, or Africa. Even in its greatest period Arabic literature was closed to influence from the Christian world. True, the *Falasifa* had learned what they could from Greek philosophy; but only because they saw Greek philosophy as adding a crucial metaphysical dimension to the message of the Koran. While Marguerite de Navarre and Boccaccio were discovering and retelling the tales of Arabia, while Langland and Chaucer were responding in their poetry to what they understood of Averroës and Avicenna, Arabic thought and literature continued as though nothing important could possibly occur outside the *dar al-islam*.

Moreover, it is only a very narrow view of our artistic tradition that does not discover in it a multicultural approach that is far more imaginative than anything that is now taught under that name. Our culture invokes a historical community of sentiment while celebrating universal human values. It is rooted in the Christian experience, but draws from that source a wealth of human feeling that it spreads impartially over imagined worlds. From *Orlando Furioso* and *Don Quixote* to Byron's *Don Juan,* from Monteverdi's *Poppeia* to Longfellow's *Hiawatha,* from *The Winter's Tale* to *Madama Butterfly* and *Das Lied von der Erde,* our culture has continuously ventured into spiritual territory that has no place on the Christian map. Those great aesthetic achievements belong with the secular rule of law, territorial jurisdiction, and the aspiration towards citizenship as products of the loyalties that enable men and women to identify in imagination with those from "elsewhere."

The culture of repudiation marks a crumbling of Enlightenment in other ways. As is frequently remarked, the spirit of free inquiry is now disappearing from schools and universities in the West. Books are put on or struck off the curriculum on grounds of political correctness; speech codes and counseling services police the language and conduct of both students and teachers; many courses are designed to impart ideological conformity rather than to inspire rational inquiry, and students are often penalized for having drawn some heretical conclusion about the leading issues of the day. In sensitive areas, such as the study of race and sex, censorship is overtly directed not only at students but also at any teacher, however impartial and scrupulous, who comes up with the wrong conclusions. "Racism awareness courses" on the American campus are often used as "correctives"—i.e., punishments—for those whose deviant behavior calls for re-education. The culture of repudiation therefore reminds us that free inquiry is not a normal exercise of the human mind, and is attractive only when seen as an avenue to membership. When the experience of membership can no longer be obtained in such a way, a new kind of inquiry takes over, one explicitly directed towards a promised social goal.

A single theme runs through the humanities as they are regularly taught in American and European universities: the illegitimacy of Western civilization, and the artificial nature of the distinctions on which it has been based. All distinctions are "cultural," therefore "constructed," therefore "ideological," in the sense defined by Marx—manufactured by the ruling classes in order to serve their interests and bolster their power. Western civilization is simply the record of that oppressive process, and the principal purpose of studying it is to deconstruct its claim to our membership. This is the core belief that a great many students in the humanities are required to ingest, preferably before they have the intellectual discipline to question it, or to set it against the literature that shows it to be untenable.

To put the point in another way: the Enlightenment displaced theology from the heart of the curriculum in order to put the disinterested pursuit of truth in its place. Within a very short time, however, we find the university dominated by theology of another kind—a godless theology, to be sure, but no less insistent upon unquestioning submission to doctrine, and no less ardent in its pursuit of heretics, skeptics, and debunkers. Of course, people are no longer burned at the stake for their views: they simply fail to get tenure or, if they are students, flunk a course.

Aristotle told us that all human beings desire to know; but he failed to point out that they do so only when first reassured that knowledge will not be dangerous. People turn from uncomfortable truths, and construct walls that will make those truths imperceptible. It is difficult to construct such a wall on your own; but, in partnership with others, and protected by a well-endowed institution, you can participate in the joyous work of falsehood, and add your own block of adamantine prose to the ramparts. The purpose is not to tell lies, but to create an acceptable *public doctrine*. And a public doctrine is acceptable if it provides the foundation for a stable and internally secure human community. In short, the vast changes in the cultural life of Western societies have their origin in the search for membership among people for whom the old loyalties have lost their appeal.

In place of the old beliefs of a civilization based on

godliness, judgment, and historical loyalty, young people are given the new beliefs of a society based on equality and inclusion, and are told that the judgment of other lifestyles is a crime. If the purpose were merely to substitute one belief system for another it would be open to rational debate. But the purpose is to substitute one *community* for another. The project is also a negative one—to sever young people from historical loyalties that have lost their moral and religious dynamism. The "non-judgmental" attitude towards other cultures goes hand-in-hand with a fierce denunciation of the culture that might have been one's own—something that we have witnessed repeatedly among the American opinion-forming elites since September 11. Unfortunately, however, there is no such thing as a community based in repudiation. The assault on the old cultural inheritance leads to no new form of membership, but only to a kind of alienation.

The poet Robert Bly argues that we have entered a "sibling society" in which relations to parents lose all significance amid the sidelong glances to one's contemporaries and peers.[19] That description strikes a chord, but in itself it is no diagnosis. Why does this society exist? Why is there a "culture of youth," and why does this culture define itself negatively, in opposition to the loyalties and pieties of parents? The answer lies surely in the mounting religious deficit in modern societies—the disappearance of the rites of passage and forms of submission that grant, at the end of the long hard road of adolescence, the transition to a higher state of membership.[20] When religious faith evaporates, when adults cease to induct young people into the national culture, when loyalties no longer stretch across generations or define themselves in territorial terms, then inevitably the society of strangers, held together by citizenship, is under threat. Young people confront a moral void. Either they reach for some new form of loyalty, like the members of al-Muhajiroun, or they obliterate the demands of society entirely, through a collective dissipation of the will to inherit—a dissipation that is both cause and effect of the sex-and-drugs lifestyle of the modern teenager.

It is tempting to liken humanity to a herd perambulating in some gloomy valley, where the warm smell of collective life provides a refuge from anxiety. Every now and then the herd emerges onto a hilltop and is suddenly bathed in the rays of the sun. Cool breezes scatter the scent of fellowship, but for a while the true nature of mankind is visible. A few individuals try to stay aloft, enjoying the light and the knowledge that it brings. But the rest are troubled by the breezes and the herd moves on, dragging everyone downhill into darkness.

Such is the situation in which we find ourselves. We are products of Enlightenment, living through the decline in the form of membership on which Enlightenment depends, and prey to the superstitions that arise in the wake of our crumbling orthodoxies. At the same time we enjoy unprecedented technological powers, which are compelling a constant acceleration of contacts and trade across the globe. People are being brought into connection who have no real way of accommodating one another, and the spectacle of Western freedom and Western prosperity, going hand-in-hand with Western decadence and the crumbling of Western loyalties, is bound to provoke, in those who envy the one and despise the other, a seething desire to punish.

CHAPTER 3

HOLY LAW

IN THE LAST CHAPTER I argued that the Western idea of citizenship is dependent upon a territorial jurisdiction, which in turn requires pre-political loyalties of a territorial and national kind. I also suggested that these loyalties are breaking down, repudiated by those whose role it is to transmit them, and unsupported by traditional ties. The unsatisfied religious need of Western societies coincides with a process of globalization that spreads the message of Western decadence around the world. In this chapter I try to understand the impact of that message on the Muslim conscience, and the impact of Islam on people now living in the West.

Islam is rapidly adding to the number of its adherents, and only 20 percent of Muslims are now Arabs—i.e., native speakers of the Arabic language and heirs to its culture. Moreover some 5 to 10 percent of Arabs are Christians, and in recent times Christian Arabs have played a disproportionate role in the revival of Arabic literature.[1] In modern conditions, therefore, it would be a gross

mistake to identify Islam with Arabic culture, or to believe that a full understanding of Islamic thought and
politics can be obtained merely from a study of the Middle
East. At the same time, the faith, law, and worldview of
the Muslim diaspora directly derives from a text whose
meaning and emotional weight are contained within its
language, and that language is Arabic. Although there
arose, in the wake of the Koran, an extraordinary civilization, and a literary and artistic culture that matched those
of contemporary Europe, the principal source of Islamic
cultural achievements is the single book from which the
faith began. The early Muslims were influenced by the
Christian and Jewish tribes with whom they shared, or
fought for, territory. The early medieval Islamic philosophers were heavily influenced by Greek philosophy. And
the Shi'ites of the classical period took much from the
literary traditions of Persia and the ornamental art of India. Nevertheless, foreign inputs into Islam have never
diminished or qualified the original vision, whose power—
inseparably attached to chant and prayer and ritual—continues unaltered in the modern world. Although I have
space only for the briefest summary, I take comfort in the
fact that contemporary authors and scholars have eluci-
dated the territory so well that the interested reader can
easily explore the matter in depth.[2]

The student of Muslim thought will be struck by
how narrowly the classical thinkers pondered the problems of political order, and how sparse and theological are

their theories of institutions. Apart from the caliphate—
the office of "successor to" or "substitute for" the Prophet—
no human institution occupies such thinkers as Al-
Mawardi, Al-Ghazali, Ibn Taymiya, or Saif Ibn 'Umar al-
Asadi for long, and discussions of sovereignty—*sultan,
mulk*—tend to be exhortatory, instructions for the ruler
that will help him to guide his people in the ways of the
faith.[3] The *Falasifa* (i.e., thinkers influenced by Greek
philosophy) composed their intellectual agenda by syn-
thesizing the Koran with what they knew of Aristotle and
Plato (often from garbled Hellenistic sources). But the
result is a peculiarly frozen vision of the art of politics as
the Greeks had expounded it. Al-Farabi, for example,
describes the philosopher-king of Plato as the prophet,
lawgiver, and *imam* to his community, suggesting indeed
that "the meaning of *imam*, philosopher, and lawgiver is
one and the same."[4] He emphasizes the distinction between reason and revelation, as pondered by the contemporary Mu'tazili school of theologians, who held that
reason could supplement the revelations provided by the
Prophet. And he acknowledged the possibility of a political system based purely on reason and directed to the
earthly needs of the citizens. But the true system, he
insists, is founded in revelation, and directed towards
happiness in the world to come. Ibn Sina (Avicenna)
likewise gives precedence to revelation, and his ideal state
is founded on prophecy and guided by the immutable
shari'a. The constitution of such a state is prophetically

revealed, and is "our Sunna which was sent down from heaven."[5]

Law is fundamental to Islam, since the religion grew from Muhammad's attempt to give an abiding code of conduct to his followers. Hence arose the four surviving schools (known as *madhahib,* or sects) of jurisprudence, with their subtle devices (*hila*) for discovering creative solutions within the letter (though not always the spirit) of the law.[6] These four schools (*Hanafi, Hanbali, Shafi* and *Maliki*, named for their founders) are accepted by each other as legitimate, but may produce conflicting judgments in any particular case. As a result the body of Islamic jurisprudence (the *fiqh*) is now enormous. Such legal knowledge notwithstanding, discussions of the *nature* of law, the grounds of its legitimacy, and the distinguishing marks of legal, as opposed to coercive, social structures are minimalist. Classical Islamic jurisprudence, like classical Islamic philosophy, assumes that law originates in divine command, as revealed through the Koran and the Sunna, and as deduced by analogy (*qiyas*) or consensus (*ijma'*). Apart from these four sources (*usul*) of law, no other source is recognized. Law, in other words, is the will of God, and sovereignty is legitimate only in so far as it upholds God's will and is authorized through it.

There is nevertheless one great classical thinker who addressed the realities of social order, and the nature of the power exerted through it, in secular rather than theological terms: Ibn Khaldun, the fourteenth-century Tunisian polymath whose *Muqaddimah* is a kind of prolegomenon to the study of history and offers a general perspective on the rise and decline of human societies. Ibn Khaldun's primary subject of study had been the Bedouin societies of North Africa; but he generalized also from his knowledge of Muslim history. Societies, he argued, are held together by a cohesive force, which he called *'asabiya* (*'asaba*, "to bind," *'asab*, a "nerve," "ligament," or "sinew"—cf. Latin *religio*). In tribal communities *'asabiya* is strong, and creates resistance to outside control, to taxation, and to government. In cities, the seat of government, *'asabiya* is weak or non-existent, and society is held together by force exerted by the ruling dynasty. But dynasties too need *'asabiya* if they are to maintain their power. Hence they inevitably decline, softened by the luxury of city life, and within four generations will be conquered by outsiders who enjoy the dynamic cohesion of the tribe.

That part of Ibn Khaldun's theory is still influential: Malise Ruthven, for example, believes that it casts light on the contemporary Muslim world, in which *'asabiya* rather than institutions remains the principal cohesive force.[7] But Ibn Khaldun's secular theory of society dwells on pre-political unity rather than political order. His actual political theory is far more Islamic in tone. Ibn Khaldun introduces a distinction between two kinds of government—that founded on religion (*siyasa diniya*) and that founded on reason (*siyasa 'aqliya*), echoing the thoughts of the Mu'tazili theologians.[8] The second form of government is more political and less theocratic, since its laws do not rest on divine authority but on rational principles that can be understood and accepted without the benefit of faith. But Ibn Khaldun finds himself unable to approve of this form of politics. Secular law, he argues, leads to a decline of 'asabiya, such as occurred when the Islamic *umma* passed from Arab to Persian rule. Moreover the impediment (*wazi'*) that constrains us to abide by the law is, in the rational state, merely external. In the state founded on the *shari'a* this impediment is internal, operating directly on the will of the subject. In short, the emergence of secular politics from the prophetic community is a sign not of civilized progress but of moral decline.

In fact, Ibn Khaldun is rare among Muslim philosophers in seeing the political as a separate form of human life, with its own laws (*qawanin siyasiya*), aspirations, and procedures. His bleak view of political order is due to his bleak view of the city generally. Without the pre-political 'asabiya, cities inevitably decay, and although 'asabiya grows spontaneously in the tribal communities of the countryside, it is loosened by the ease and luxury of city life. Ibn Khaldun anticipated the "culture of repudiation" that I described in the last chapter, although he gave it no such name. But his underlying purpose was to distinguish the caliphate (*khilafa*), which had persisted during the reign of the four "righteous" caliphs who succeeded the Prophet in Arabia, from the worldly sovereignty (*mulk*) that had gradually replaced it. Only the caliphate, in Ibn Khaldun's eyes, had either the right or the power to survive the collapse of earthly dynasties, and Muslims must work constantly to restore it as the rule of God on earth.

For all his subtlety, therefore, Ibn Khaldun ends by endorsing the traditional, static idea of government according to the *shari'a*. To put in a nutshell what is distinctive about this traditional idea of government: the Muslim conception of law as holy law, pointing the unique way to salvation, and applying to every area of human life, involves a *confiscation of the political*. Those matters which, in Western societies, are resolved by negotiation, compromise, and the laborious work of offices and committees are the object of immovable and eternal decrees, either laid down explicitly in the holy book, or discerned there by some religious figurehead—whose authority, however, can always be questioned by some rival *imam* or jurist, since the *shari'a* recognizes no office or institution as endowed with any independent lawmaking power.

Three features of the original message embodied in the Koran have proved decisive in this respect. First, the Messenger of God was presented with the problem of organizing and leading an autonomous community of followers. Unlike Jesus, he was not a religious visionary operating under an all-embracing imperial law, but a political leader, inspired by a revelation of God's purpose and determined to assert that purpose against the surrounding world of tribal government and pagan superstition.

Second, the suras of the Koran make no distinction

between the public and the private spheres: what is commanded to the believers is commanded in response to the many problems, great and small, that emerged during the course of Muhammad's political mission. But each command issues from the same divine authority. Laws governing marriage, property, usury, and commerce occur side-by-side with rules of domestic ritual, good manners, and personal hygiene. The conduct of war and the treatment of criminals are dealt with in the same tone of voice as diet and defecation. The whole life of the community is set out in a disordered, but ultimately consistent, set of absolutes, and it is impossible to judge from the text itself whether any of these laws is more important, more threatening, or more dear to God's heart than the others. The opportunity never arises, for the student of the Koran, to distinguish those matters which are open to political negotiation from those which are absolute duties to God. In effect, everything is owed to God, with the consequence that nothing is owed to Caesar.

Third, the social vision of the Koran is shaped through and through by the tribal order and commercial dealings of Muhammad's Arabia. It is a vision of people bound to each other by family ties and tribal loyalties, but answerable for their actions to God alone. No mention is made of institutions, corporations, societies, or procedures with any independent authority. Life, as portrayed in the Koran, is a stark, unmediated confrontation between the individual and his God, in which the threat of punishment and the hope of reward are never far from the thoughts of either party.

Therefore, although the Koran is the record of a political project, it lays no foundations for an impersonal political order, but vests all power and authority in the Messenger of God. There are no provisions for the Messenger's successor, or even for the priesthood. The office of *imam*—the one who "stands in front," i.e., who leads the community in prayer—was assumed by Muhammad until the day when illness prevented him from performing it and he asked his father-in-law Abu Bakr to perform the office in his stead (Abu Bakr was subsequently chosen as the first Caliph, on account of the special favor shown to him by the Prophet).

It is still true that an *imam* has no institutional authority in the Sunni tradition, and is merely a man whose personal qualities and religious knowledge fit him for the role. The title of Imam is reserved by the Shi'ites for Muhammad's first cousin 'Ali and his descendants, who are regarded as the true successors of the Prophet. But even in the Shi'ite tradition, there is no conception of a priestly office that confers authority upon the one who holds it: authority is bestowed directly by the power of God. This point is made further evident by the fact that, according to the Shi'ites, the line of *imams* ceased after the twelfth, who is the still living "hidden" imam, destined to reappear in the last days as the *mahdi* or "Director," and who, according to the Koran, will announce the Day of

Judgment. Hence no living cleric can act with any greater authority than that conferred by his own personal qualities in the eyes of God—unless he can show himself actually to *be* the hidden *imam*, revealed at last after centuries of divine displeasure, a feat that Khomeini set out to accomplish, but with only transient success.

The office of Caliph began as an attempt to recapture a vanished personal authority. Hence Caliphs repeatedly failed to give proof of their legitimacy, and the first three of them began a lengthy tradition by dying at the hands of assassins. Those who rule in the Prophet's name seldom satisfy their subjects that they are entitled to do so, since the authority that is looked for in an Islamic ruler is—to use Weber's idiom—a charismatic, rather than a legal-rational, form.[9] Islamic revivals almost always begin from a sense of the corruption and godlessness of the ruling power, and a desire to rediscover the holy leader who will restore the pure way of life that had been laid down by the Prophet. There seems to be no room in Islamic thinking for the idea—vital to the history of Western constitutional government—of an office that works for the benefit of the community, regardless of the virtues and vices of the one who fills it. Spinoza put the point explicitly by arguing that what makes for excellence in the state is not that it should be governed by good men, but that it should be so constituted that it does not matter whether it be governed by good men or bad.[10] This idea goes back to Aristotle, and is the root of political order in the Western tradition—the government of laws, not of men, *even though it is men who make the laws*. There seems to be no similar idea in Islamic political thinking, since institutions, offices, and collective entities play no part in securing political legitimacy, and all authority stems from God, via the words, deeds, and example of his Messenger.

The reader of the Koran will be struck by the radical change of tone that the revelations exhibit after the Prophet has been forced into exile at Medina. The early Meccan suras (most of which occur at the end of the book in the now canonical ordering) are short, intensely lyrical, and written in a free rhyming prose that echoes the style of the pagan poets of Muhammad's Arabia. They invoke the natural world and the wonderful signs of its Creator, being hymns of praise to the single omnipotent God who speaks directly to his worshippers, and who is revealed in all things. They are the great dawn-vision of an impassioned monotheist, from whose soul oppressive shadows are being chased away.

The Medina suras are much longer, often tetchy and cantankerous, although punctuated from time to time by poetic invocations in the Meccan style. They deal with the trials and tribulations of leadership, and the revelations are often granted as concrete responses to the problems of communal life. Muhammad's project is revealed at every step, and it is a remarkable one: to replace the tribal society and its pagan gods with a new, universal order—the Islamic *umma*—founded on belief in the one true God and on the acceptance of his commands. To achieve this result Muhammad had to persuade people that he was God's messenger; he had also to give proof of God's favor by success in war.

Although the community at Medina had escaped from its persecutors, it retained a powerful sense of belonging elsewhere. They were *al-muhajiroun*, the ones in emigration or exile (*hijrah*), and the experience of exile is invoked again and again in the Islamic revivals of our times—not least by the British group linked to al-Qaʻeda and called al-Muhajiroun. The absolute tone of command of the Medina suras therefore goes hand-in-hand with an intense nostalgia, and it is not surprising that the idea of pilgrimage to the distant home should have rooted itself in Muhammad's mind to become one "pillar" (*rukn*) among the five that constitute the core duties of the Muslim. (The other pillars [*arkan*] are: the *shahada* or bearing witness [namely, that there is no god but Allah and that Muhammad is his Prophet]; the *salat,* or liturgical prayer; the *zakat*, or obligatory charity; and the *sawm*, or annual fast, of Ramadan.) And incorporated into the rites of pilgrimage are the ritual obeisances before the Kabʻah, the pagan temple whose black stone Muhammad had worshipped as a child, and whose rites helped to shape the liturgy that Muhammad subsequently devised for his own community.

I mention this point because it helps to explain how alien the Koranic vision of society is to any idea of territorial jurisdiction or national loyalty. In the eyes of the Koran the place where we are is not the place where we belong, since the place where we belong is *in the wrong hands*: Our law therefore does not issue from our present place of abode, and gives special privileges only to the other place, which may one day be reconquered. This attitude greatly favors the notion of law as a relation between each person and God, with no special reference to territory, sovereignty, or worldly obedience. Although localities are of enormous importance in the Muslim worldview it is not because they are the *sources* of law but because they are the *object* of law, declared holy by God in his eternal dealings with mankind. A holy place is precisely one subsumed into the divine order of things, rather than the seat, like Rome or Paris, of a territorial jurisdiction. This is of great significance in the current conflict over Jerusalem, which for the Muslim is a place set apart from its earthly surroundings just as Mecca is set apart, scarcely belonging to the geography of the actual world but existing in the numinous region of divine imperatives. Hence the name of Jerusalem in Arabic—*al-Quds*, or "the holy (city)."

After the initial turmoils—in which the conflict between two of the righteous Caliphs, 'Uthman and 'Ali, led to the split between Sunni and Shi'ite—the Muslim dynasties gained territory by conquest. The caliphate emerged as a genuine institution, though one increasingly deprived of political power. Nevertheless, the experience of settled government led to serious attempts by learned men to adapt the faith to the needs of government. This was the great period of the hadiths—traditions, authenticated by pious examination, which recorded such words and deeds of the Prophet as might offer guidance to a settled community. These hadiths are markedly more peaceful and conciliatory than the Medina suras, and have clearly been shaped by the experience of a society in which charismatic leadership is no longer the norm. They are an attempt to read back into the prophetic source of Islam the real achievements of Islamic forms of government. At the same time there arose the four schools of *fiqh,* which bring together the reflections of jurists over generations, and show the attempt by *ijtihad* to establish a genuine rule of law in places where law is nevertheless seen as issuing placelessly and timelessly from the will of God.

Even in that great period of jurisprudence, however, the *shari'a* remained defective in the crucial matter of legal personality. As Malise Ruthven has pointed out, there is no provision in Islamic law for the corporation as a legal person, with rights and duties of its own.[11] The city, the committee, the mosque itself, do not occur as independent subjects of the law, and although Muslim countries abound in charitable foundations—the *awqaf* (singular *waqf*)—they are conceived not as property in the hands of a corporate person, but as property that has been simply "removed" from circulation or has "ceased" (*waqafa*). In Ruthven's words, there was no "juridical definition of the public sphere" in classical Islamic jurisprudence,[12] a fact that greatly impeded the formation of a genuine political order. Hence "stealing from the public treasury was not held subject to the *hadd* [i.e., divinely ordained] punishment for theft, because the illegal act was not committed against a juristic agent independent of the thief who was, along with every other Muslim, considered part-owner of the *mal Allah*, and thus part-owner of what he had stolen."[13]

Two momentous consequences follow from the adoption of the *shari'a*. First, because it is a law governing only Muslims, the *shari'a* leaves the status of other communities undefined. These other communities remain strictly "outside the law," and must either convert or accept the status of *dhimma*—which means protected by treaty or covenant. Only "people of the book"—i.e., Jews, Christians, and (in Persia) Zoroastrians—have traditionally been accorded this status. *Dhimma* is offered in return for the payment of taxes, and grants no clear and justiciable rights apart from a general right of protection.[14] Although free communities of Christians and Jews often thrived under Islamic law, there was no formal or legal acceptance of their right to worship in their own manner, and their property was subject to confiscation on more or less arbitrary grounds. The Turkish *millet* system rectified this, but depended for its authority on the secular rule of the Sultan, and had no authority in the *shari'a*.

Second, the way of life that grows under the aegis of the *shari'a* is profoundly domestic, without any public or ceremonial character except in the matter of communal worship. The mosque and its school, or *madrasah*, together with the *souq* or bazaar, are the only genuine public spaces in traditional Muslim towns. The street is a lane among private houses, which lie along it and across it in a disorderly jumble of inward-turning courtyards. The Muslim city is a creation of the *shari'a*—a hive of private spaces, built cell on cell. Above its rooftops the minarets point to God like outstretched fingers, resounding with the voice of the muezzin as he calls the faithful to prayer.

I mention these two features because they are often overlooked, despite their enormous importance in the psychology and the politics of the Islamic world. The Muslim city is explicitly a city for Muslims, a place of congregation in which individuals and their families live side-by-side in obedience to God, and where non-Muslims exist only on sufferance. The mosque is the link to God, and pious people believe that no building should overtop the minarets, or destroy their mastery of the skyline. The true city lies huddled under God's protection, and even the finest palace is no more than a private chamber, ordered by family rituals and sanctified by prayer.

The image of such a city is familiar to all of us from the *Thousand and One Nights*, and also from the engravings and sketches of nineteenth-century travellers. And here and there the Muslim city still exists, ravaged by the modern styles of building and by the densely crowded jerry-built slums, but the image, for the ordinary believer, of a communal form of peace. Many a Muslim carries this image in his heart, and when he encounters the Western city, with its open spaces and public buildings, its wide streets, its visible interiors, its skyscrapers dwarfing the few religious buildings, and its high-rises in alloy and glass, he is apt to feel both wonder and rage at the God-defying arrogance that has so completely eclipsed the life of piety and prayer. It is not merely of anecdotal significance that, when Mohammed Atta left his native Egypt for Hamburg to continue his studies in architecture, it was not to learn about the modernist buildings that disfigure German cities, but to write a thesis on the restoration of the ancient city of Aleppo, where the philosopher al-Farabi once resided in the court of a Hamdanid prince.[15] When he led the attack against the World Trade Center, Atta was assaulting a symbol of economic, aesthetic, and spiritual paganism.

The image of the Muslim city belongs with the intense nostalgia that is generic to the Muslim faith. This nostalgia is fed by the incantatory language of the Koran, by the stories of the Prophet, by the constant reverence towards the distant holy place where the Prophet once lived, and which he commanded his followers to visit. It is also fed by the manifest corruption that pervades the Islamic world, by the catastrophic and disorienting demographic changes that have so altered the landscape, the cities, and the pace of life in that world, and by forms of government that seem to deprive the ordinary Muslim of a voice.

It has often been said that Islam has turned its back on modernity, which it cannot encompass through its law and doctrine. And to some extent this is true, the efforts of Westernizers and legal reformers notwithstanding. Much more important, however, is the intense longing for that original and pure community once promised by the Prophet but betrayed over and again by his worldly successors and followers. Like every form of nostalgia, this longing involves a turning away from reality, a refusal to accommodate or even to perceive the facts that might undermine it, and an endlessly renewable anger against the Other who refuses to share in the collective dream. Nowhere is this more evident than in the revived Shi'ism of the Ayatollah Khomeini, which channels into the destructive longing to remake the world a tradition of lamentation that makes human sacrifice into the primary avenue to sainthood.

At the same time this nostalgic faith can make an enormous contribution to the happiness of those who adopt it. Those who see religion simply as a set of doctrines concerning the origin of the world, the laws that govern it, and the destiny of mankind will think of faith merely as a substitute for rational argument, destined to crumble before the advance of science or to persist, if at all, as a jumble of tattered superstitions in the midst of a world that refutes them. But doctrine is the least important part of religion, as Muhammad—with a penetrating genius matched by few religious leaders before or since—came quickly to see. Communities are not formed by doctrine, but by obedience, and the two great instruments for securing obedience are ritual and law. The Muslim faith involves constant rehearsal of the believer's submission to God. The repetition of sacred words and formulae, the exact performance of gestures whose only explanation is that they have been commanded, the obligatory times of prayer (where prayer is a fervent but simple acknowledgement of God's greatness, of the special position of his Prophet, and of the Day of Judgment, which only the righteous need not fear), the annual fast and all the duties required by it, the dietary laws, the pilgrimage to Mecca with its myriad obligatory actions—all this, which is meaningless to the skeptical outsider, is the stuff of consolation.[16] Ritual places people on a plane of absolute equality; it overcomes distance, extinguishes the self in the flow of collective emotion, and—by offering absolute commands that can be obeyed without trouble—refreshes the worshipper with a sense that he has regained favor in God's sight and hence his place in the community of believers. Ritual is a discipline of the body that conveys and reinforces a discipline of the soul. It is the outward manifestation of the collective act of submission (*islam*) that unites the community of believers. And it is one undeniable source of the peace and gentleness of the old Muslim city.

In short, Islam offers an unparalleled form of membership, and one whose appeal is all the greater in that it transcends time and place, joining the believer to a universal *umma* whose only sovereign is God. Even if it may appear, to the skeptical modernist, as a medieval fossil, Islam has an unrivalled ability to compensate for what is lacking in modern experience. It rationalizes and validates the condition of exile: the condition in which we all find ourselves, severed by the hectic motion of mechanized life from the age-old experience of membership. Nothing evokes this more clearly than the collective rite in which the faithful turn to Mecca with their prayers—projecting their submission and their longing away from the place where they are to that other and holy place where they are not, and whose contours are defined not by geography but by religious need.

Islam, in other words, is less a theological doctrine than a system of *piety*. To submit to it is to discover the rules for a trouble-free life and an easy conscience. Moreover, rooted in the ritual and taking constant nourishment from it is a system of morality that clarifies those matters which must be clarified if people are to live with each other in peace. It is a system that safeguards the family as the primary object of loyalty and trust; that clarifies and disciplines sexual conduct; that sanctifies ordinary obligations of friendship and kinship; and that lays down rules for business that have a power to exonerate as well as to blame. Even if this morality, like the rituals that feed it, has its origin in the long vanished pastoral communities of Arabia, even if it threatens those freedoms which Westerners take for granted and which the rising generation of

Muslim immigrants wish to exploit, it has the singular advantage, in the modern context, of clarity. It tells the faithful what they must do in order to be on good terms with God; and what they must do is entirely a matter of private life, ritual, and worship. The public sphere can be left to look after itself, and the ordinary Muslim has no need to be concerned with it.[17] In the context of Western *anomie* and self-indulgence, therefore, Muslim immigrants cling to their faith, seeing it inevitably as something superior to the surrounding moral chaos, and therefore more worthy of obedience than the law that permits so much sin. Their children may rebel for a while against the strict sexual codes and patriarchal absolutes of the Muslim family; but they too, in any crisis, are drawn to their ancestral faith, which offers a vision of blamelessness and moral security they find nowhere in the public space Western political systems have devoted themselves to generating.

Furthermore, we should recognize the immense importance of the *madrasah* in providing young people with a loyalty and a rite of passage that they can no longer easily obtain from our own secular schools. Backward though Islamic education may seem, when judged in terms of free inquiry and scientific rigor, it is vastly superior, from the moral and cultural point of view, to the education now available to a great many young people in Western cities. It teaches piety, consideration, and respect for age; it offers a clear rite of passage into the adult world; it presents the student at every point with certainties rather than doubts, and consolation rather than anxiety. It also promotes the study of classical Arabic, and leads the student to commit vast amounts of a great and dignified text to memory, so providing what most modern people lack to their detriment—namely, a repertoire of quotations, maxims, and well-crafted sayings upon which to draw in one's daily life and relationships. These fragments of a text imbued with certainty are precious to those who study them, and serve to elevate the believer's thoughts and feelings so far above the banal level of the TV sitcom or the pop-music video that he can, without effort, see those products of Western materialism for the rubbish that they are. In short, it is an education that provides what the liberal systems of education in Western states have, disastrously, despised—authority.

This advantage of Islamic education is not diminished by the fact that the Islamic tradition of learning has all but disappeared from the modern world. The education of the *madrasah* provides a common culture, rather than a high culture.[18] It is egalitarian, uncritical, and focused on essentials. And it is taught without reference to the high culture of medieval Islam, which has no real standing in the countries where it grew. This situation is the reverse of that which prevails in the West today. The education offered by our schools does not impart a common culture; it gives little guidance for life, few certainties, and unequal skills. But those who can take advantage of the surrounding freedom can quickly avail themselves of a high culture, philosophy, and open debate in which ignorance is not exalted but despised.

In other words, Western societies provide a public space that compensates for educational decline by offering the freedom to grow and to learn in other ways. But this public space does not exist in traditional Islamic society. The writ of holy law runs through all things, and the idea that there should be a zone of freedom and experiment protected by a law purely human in its origins, and sustained by a political process in which human choices are the ultimate source of legitimacy, is alien to Islam. This does not mean that Islamic societies have been governed solely by the *shari'a*. On the contrary, in almost all respects relevant to the government of a large society, the *shari'a* is radically deficient. It proceeds by the application of immensely complex sources to the individual case and, while rich in jurisprudential commentary, has produced no body of general laws.

It has therefore been necessary at every epoch for the ruler—whether Caliph or Sultan, Emir, Khedif, or President—to lay down laws of his own that will guarantee his power, facilitate administration, and permit the collection of taxes. But these laws have no independent legitimacy in the eyes of those compelled to obey them. They do not create a space outside religion in which freedom is the norm. On the contrary, they merely add to the constraints of the holy law the rules of a political order that is backed by no *de jure* authority, but only by *de facto* power. In any upheaval they are rejected entirely as the arbitrary edicts of a usurper. Hence, there is no scope in a traditional Islamic society for the kinds of purely political development, through the patient building of institutions and secular laws, that we know in the West. Change, when it comes, takes the form of a crisis, as power is challenged from below in the name of the one true Power above.

If the only way in which a law can be legitimated is by deriving it from a command of God, then clearly all secular laws are seen as mere expedients adopted by the ruler. In such circumstances it is unlikely that any kind of constitutional, representative, or democratic government will emerge or achieve stability. Secular government will be either an arm of the imperial power, as under the Ottoman Empire, or a vestige of the same, as in much of the Middle East today. Although the Ottoman Empire attempted reforms that would give legitimacy to its centralized administration, these reforms—which led first to the destruction of the Empire, and then to the emergence of the modern Turkish state under Mustafah Kemal Atatürk— were explicitly "Westernizing," involving both a deliberate move away from Islamic ideas of legitimacy, and a ruthless secularization of society, with the *'ulama'* losing whatever power they had once possessed in the educational, legal, and administrative processes.

The Westernizing of Turkey was made possible by its imperial history, which had imposed the obligation to govern distant provinces and recalcitrant tribes by a system of law that could only here and there be justified by some divine genealogy and which was therefore constantly seeking legitimacy of another kind. By remaking Turkey as a territorial, rather than an imperial, power, and by simultaneously secularizing and Turkifying the Ottoman culture, Atatürk created a national loyalty, a territorial jurisdiction, and a form of constitutional government. As a consequence, Turkey has been the only durable democracy in the Muslim world—although a democracy maintained as such by frequent interventions by an army loyal to the Kemalist project. This transition has not been without cost, however. Modern Turkey has been effectively severed from its past and its classical culture by social and linguistic reforms that have made the traditional literature of the country unreadable to all except the specialist scholar. And in the ensuing search for a modern identity, young people are repeatedly attracted to radical and destabilizing ideologies, both Islamist and utopian.

This search for identity takes another but related form in the Arabic-speaking countries, and the al-Qaʿeda organization should be understood as one significant result of it.[19] Of course, terrorism of the al-Qaʿeda kind is an abnormality, repudiated by the majority of Muslims. It would be the greatest injustice to confuse Islam, as a pious way of life, with contemporary Islamism, which is an example of what Burke, writing of the French Revolutionaries, called an "armed doctrine"[20]—in other words a belligerent ideology bent on eradicating all opposition to its claims. Nevertheless, Islamism is not an accidental product of the crisis that Islam is currently undergoing, and the fundamental tenets of the faith must be borne in mind by those who wish to understand the terrorist movements.[21]

Al-Qaʿeda is the personal creation of Osama bin Laden; but it derives from three pre-existing sociopolitical forces: the Wahhabite movement in Saudi Arabia; the Muslim Brotherhood that emerged in modern Egypt; and, finally, the technological education now available to disaffected Muslims throughout the Middle East.

The Wahhabite movement has its roots in the sect (*madhhab*) founded by Ahmad Ibn Hanbal (780–855), whose collection of 30,000 hadiths, allegedly selected from 750,000 contenders, formed the basis of the Hanbali *fiqh*. The leading principle of Hanbali jurisprudence is that law should not be formalized in rules or maxims but constantly derived afresh from the original sources by an effort (*ijtihad*) that renews both the faith and the understanding of the judge. Hence Muslims must be constantly returned to the Koran and the words of the Prophet, the authority of which cannot be overridden by political decrees or formal legal systems. Although Hanbalism has always been recognized as a legitimate school of *fiqh*, its uncompromising emphasis on the origins of the Muslim faith has made it a permanent source of opposition to the established powers in Muslim countries. Hence, when Muhammad Ibn ʿAbd al-Wahhab (1691–1765), a native of Najd, the central province of Arabia, sought to restore the true faith to the Prophet's sacred territory, he expressed himself in Hanbali terms. The aim was to return from the corrupt practices that flourished under the Ottoman Empire and its factititous rules and offices to the original teachings of the Prophet and his Companions. Compelled to seek asylum in Deraiah, al-Wahhab attracted the local chieftain, Muhammad Ibn Sa'ud, to his cause. And it was Ibn Sa'ud's grandson who, with a fanatical and puritanical following, "liberated" Mecca from the idolatrous practices that had rooted themselves there, establishing at the same time a short-lived kingdom in Arabia, and thereafter paying for his presumption with his life.

Despite this political failure, Wahhabism took root in the Arabian peninsula. The Wahhabis preached purity of lifestyle and absolute obedience to the Koran, free from all compromise with the *dar al-harb*. They rejected the official schools of *fiqh*, including the Hanbali *madhhab* that had inspired their founder, and argued that whoever can read the Koran can judge for himself in matters of doctrine. After the death of the Companions, therefore, no new consensus (*ijma'*) could be admitted. The message of the Wahhabis was that of the Prophet: the unity of God. And they described themselves as *muwahhidoun*, or "Unitarians," and all others as *mushrikoun*, i.e., those who associate partners with Allah.

In the early twentieth century a group of Wahhabis gathered around a descendent of the original Ibn Sa'ud to form a brotherhood (*ikhwan*) dedicated to the re-establishment of a purified faith by *jihad*. Starting out with a handful of followers from Kuwait in 1902, Ibn Sa'ud, as the world now knows him, gradually drove the Turkish clients from their paper thrones in the Arabian peninsula. By the time that the Ottoman Empire collapsed, Ibn Sa'ud was able to declare a kingdom of Saudi Arabia in the peninsula, and for a brief while the *ikhwan* exerted their fanatical influence over the holy places, causing widespread alarm in the region. However, Ibn Sa'ud, now a player on the stage of international politics, came to see that he must negotiate with the British for the secure possession of his kingdom, and that the suppression of his following would be a necessary price.

Although the *ikhwan* were brought to heel, many of them through absorption into the Saudi National Guard, they did not forget their original intention, which was to engage in a *jihad* against the infidel. Nor did they forget that this aim had been diverted in the interests of a secular power. Instead of returning the sacred places to God, they had handed them over to an earthly sovereign, and one who had the impertinence, moreover, to name this holy territory for himself. It has never been forgotten by the puritan *'ulama'* of Saudi Arabia, therefore, that the spiritual legacy of Wahhabism has been betrayed by the family that purported to fight for it. Many of the Saudi *'ulama'* now identify themselves not as Wahhabis but as Salafis, meaning believers who remain true to the forgotten piety of the *salaf* or "ancestors" (in this context, the Companions of the

Prophet)—*al-salafiya* being another Islamic reform movement, founded in late nineteenth-century Egypt by Muhammad 'Abduh (1849–1905).

The search for that original purity, in which people are united not by political institutions but by faith and *'asabiya*, continues to exert its subterranean influence in the heartlands of Islam, breaking out in acts of violence and rebellion. One such act of rebellion—the occupation of the Sacred Mosque at Mecca by a group of *ikhwan* extremists in 1979—led to violence in the holy precinct of a kind that scandalized the entire Muslim world. The rebels were overpowered, allegedly with the help of French special forces, and executed. Thereafter dissidents drew the conclusion that no revolt will succeed against the Saudi rulers and their "imperialist" friends unless it can find a base elsewhere. Hence the importance of al-Qa'eda, whose name means "base," and which has successfully detached itself from every earthly locality, so as to threaten the Saudi dynasty from the reaches of cyberspace.

The other important Islamic movement in the formation of al-Qa'eda was also an *ikhwan*. The Muslim Brotherhood was founded in Egypt in 1928 by Hassan al-Banna, then a twenty-two-year-old elementary school teacher in Ismailia, a featureless new town named after the Khedive Ismail but controlled by the Franco-British Suez Canal Company. Surrounded on all sides by the signs and symbols of the infidel way of life, living under a jurisdiction that had lost authority in Muslim eyes and stood idly by as the Muslim way of life decayed, al-Banna, who had received a rigorous Islamic education, who had already acquired a reputation for piety, and who had been initiated into a Sufi order, responded to the appeals of his contemporaries to found a movement that would bring faith, hope, and charity to the rural migrants crowding into the shanty towns around the cities. For al-Banna, however, charity was an insufficient proof of faith: a *jihad* was also needed, which would expel the infidel from Muslim soil. Islamic clubs and discussion groups abounded in the Egypt of the time; but the Brotherhood was to be different—a return to the militant Islam of the Prophet, the goal of which would be to re-establish the reign of purity and piety that the Prophet had created in Medina.

Hassan al-Banna was profoundly influenced by the Wahhabite movement. The conquest of the Holy Places— not perhaps such a difficult matter, given the collapse of the Ottoman Empire and the devious Franco-British politics which had undermined all local authority in the region—was, for al-Banna, a triumphant proof of what could be achieved by faith, *'asabiya,* and violence. Within a decade the Brotherhood had become the best-organized indigenous political force in Egypt. Its anti-British sentiment caused it to look to the Axis powers in World War II, hoping for the liberation of Egypt and its own seizure of power thereafter. After the Allied victory, it confined itself to a campaign of terrorism, through which to "bear witness" to Islamic truth against the infidel.

This campaign was to provide the model for future Islamist movements in Iran and Lebanon. Cinemas were blown up, along with the haunts of the "infidels and heretics," while women wearing "inadequate dress" were attacked with knives. Prominent public figures were tried by the Brotherhood *in absentia* and found guilty of "causing corruption on earth": their deaths followed as a matter of course. Two prime ministers and many other high-ranking officials were murdered in this way. Young Muslims from elsewhere in the Middle East were recruited to the Brotherhood, which operated in secret, al-Banna denying all involvement in terrorism until his arrest and execution in 1949. By this time the Brotherhood had trained over a hundred terrorists from other Islamic countries, who traveled to their homelands to initiate the same kind of destabilizing mayhem that had brought chaos to Egypt. This unrest facilitated the army coup that led to the destruction of Egypt's fragile monarchy and the assumption of power by Gamal Abdul-Nasir (or Nasser, as he is generally known in the West).

The Muslim Brotherhood was outlawed and savagely repressed by Nasser. But it lived on as a secret society, proliferating through cells formed to study the letters sent from prison by its new leading personality, Sayyed Qutb (1906–66), who had lived in the United States from 1949 until 1951, and who preached the impossibility of compromise between Islam and the world of ignorance (*jahiliyya*). Qutb was a self-conscious intellectual in the

Western sense, who attempted to give Islam a decidedly modernist, even "existentialist" character. The faith of the true Muslim was, for Qutb, an expression of his innermost being against the inauthentic otherness of the surrounding world.[22] Islam was therefore the answer to the rootlessness and comfortlessness of modernity, and Qutb did not stop short of endorsing both suicide and terrorism as instruments in the self-affirmation of the believer against the *jahiliyya*. In place of the *credo quia absurdum est* of the Christian he preached the *facio quia absurdum est* (I do it because it is absurd) of the existentialist, believing that this absurdity would also be a triumph of the spirit over the surrounding pagan culture.

Qutb and hundreds of his followers were executed by Nasser in 1966, but not before their message had spread through a younger generation that was enjoying for the first time a Western-style university education and the excitement of global communications. Although Sadat and his successor, Hosni Mubarak, have tried to accommodate the Brotherhood by permitting it to reorganize as a political party, with a share in power accorded to its official leaders, the real movement continued independently, not as a form of politics, but as a form of *membership,* whose "brothers" would one day be martyrs, and who would meanwhile move among mortals, crowned by an invisible halo of ideas.

The rumor of this redemptive membership remained alive in Egypt, fostered by the Islamic university of Al-

Ahram in Cairo, and by the schools, colleges, and clubs that served the exploding population of the young. It led to the formation of a new underground *jihad*, originally under the leadership of Ayman al-Zawahiri, a wealthy surgeon. Members of this movement assassinated President Sadat in 1981, but al-Zawahiri himself was outmaneuvered in the bid for supreme command. He therefore followed the traditional path into exile, eventually joining bin Laden in Afghanistan to become the leading ideologist of al-Qa'eda. Meanwhile the *jihad* continued in Egypt, culminating in the massacre of fifty-eight tourists at Luxor in 1997.

Many of the ideological leaders of the Egyptian Islamist movement have been, like al-Zawahiri and Mohammed Atta, graduates in technical or scientific subjects. Some have had the benefit of postgraduate study in the West. Their scientific training opens to them the secrets of Western technology while at the same time revealing the emptiness of a civilization in which only technology seems to matter. Atta went as a graduate of Cairo's school of architecture, well versed in the theory and practice of modernist engineering, to the Technical University in Hamburg, there to meditate on the old Levantine city of Aleppo. Although bin Laden is a Saudi by birth, his most active followers are Egyptians, shaped by Western technology and Qutbist Islamism to become weapons in a fight to the death against technology. Al-Qa'eda offers them a new way of life that is also a way of death—an Islamist equivalent of the "being-towards-death" extolled by Heidegger, in which all external loyalties are dissolved in an act of self-sacrificial commitment.

Al-Qa'eda appeals to North African Muslims partly because it is an Arabist organization, expressing itself in the language and imagery of the Holy Koran and pursuing a conflict that has its roots in the land of the Prophet. It has given to the Sunni and Arab branch of Islamism the same sense of identity that the Shi'ite and Persian branch received from the Islamic Republic of Ayatollah Khomeini. Indeed its vision is virtually indistinguishable from that of Khomeini, who expressed it thus, in a speech delivered in December 1984:

> If one allows the infidels to continue playing their role of corrupters on Earth, their eventual moral punishment will be all the stronger. Thus, if we kill the infidels in order to put a stop to their [corrupting] activities, we have indeed done them a service. For their eventual punishment will be less. To allow the infidels to stay alive means to let them do more corrupting. [To kill them] is a surgical operation commanded by Allah the Creator. . . . Those who follow the rules of the Koran are aware that we have to apply the laws of *qissas* [retribution] and that we have to kill. . . . War is a blessing for the world and for every nation. It is Allah himself who commands men to wage war and to kill.[23]

The element of insanity in those words should not blind us to the fact that they adequately convey a mood, a legacy, and a goal that inspire young people all over the Islamic world. Moreover, although there are many passages of the Koran that could be cited in the cause of peace and reconciliation, there is no doubt that Khomeini's interpretation of the Prophet's message is capable of textual support, and that it reflects the very confiscation of the political that has been the principal feature of Islamic revolutions in the modern world.

Khomeini's sentiments do not merely reflect his reading of the Koran, however. They are the fruit of a long exile, first in Iraq and then in the West, where he was protected by the infidels whose destruction he conjures. And they are a vivid testimony to the fact that the virtues of Western political systems are, to a certain kind of Islamic mind, imperceptible—or perceptible, as they were to Qutb and Atta, only as hideous moral failings. Even while enjoying the peace, prosperity, and freedom that issue from a secular rule of law, a person who regards the *shari'a* as the unique path to salvation may see these things only as the signs of a spiritual emptiness or corruption. For someone like Khomeini, human rights and secular government display the decadence of Western civilization, which has failed to arm itself against those who intend to destroy it and hopes to appease them instead. The message is that there can be no compromise, and systems that make compromise and conciliation into their ruling principles are merely aspects of the Devil's work.

Khomeini is a figure of great historic importance for three reasons. First, he showed that Islamic government is a viable option in the modern world, so destroying the belief that Westernization and secularization are inevitable. Second, through the activities of the Hizbullah (Party of Allah) in Lebanon, he made the exportation of the Islamic Revolution the cornerstone of his foreign policy. Third, he endowed the Islamic revival with a Shi'ite physiognomy, so making martyrdom a central part of its strategy.

Islam originally spread through the world on the wings of military success. Conquest, victory, and triumph over enemies are a continual refrain of the Koran, offered as proof that God is on the side of the believers. The Shi'ites are remarkable among Muslims, however, in commemorating, as the central episode in their cult, a military defeat. To some extent they share the Christian vision of divinity as proved not through worldly triumph but through the willing acceptance of failure. Like Christians, Shi'ites take comfort in an eschatology of redemption, looking forward to the return of the Hidden Imam in the way that many Christians anticipate the Second Coming of Christ.

Hussein Ibn 'Ali, whom the Shi'ites recognize as their third Imam, was killed, together with his followers, by the armies of the Umayyad Caliph Yazid at the battle of Karbala in 680. Hussein was, for his followers, a symbol of all that is pure, innocent, and good in the Islamic way of life, and Yazid a proof that the community formed by the Prophet had fallen into the hands of corrupt and evil usurpers. By each year lamenting the defeat of Hussein, in rituals that may extend to excesses of self-inflicted injury, the Shi'ites rehearse their conviction that Islam must be constantly returned to its original purity, and that the powers that prevail in the world will always seek to corrupt it.[24] And at the same time they internalize the goal of self-sacrificial death as the final proof of merit.

This last feature became immensely important in the war against Iraq, which succeeded the Islamic Revolution in Iran. Following in the tradition of the Assassins—the followers of Hassan Sabah who terrorized the Seljuk authorities in the eleventh and twelfth centuries of our era—Khomeini issued a new call to martyrdom. Hassan Sabah had recruited an army of fedayeen (Arabic: *fida'i, fida'iyoun*, one who sacrifices himself, from *fada*, to redeem), whose mission was to kill God's enemies, and to die in the process. Khomeini's similar call to sacrifice was enthusiastically received by many young people, and even by their parents. An army of martyrs had soon been assembled, consisting largely of teenagers, who were to surrender their lives for the sake of paradise—often running across minefields to prepare the advance of professional troops. A contemporary report in the Tehran daily *Ettelaat* (30 January 1982) records one such event:

They were all volunteers. They were all aged fourteen, fifteen and sixteen to twenty. They were there to turn the minefield into a rose garden. They were blossoms in half bloom. They would rise before dawn, which is the time for roses to open up their petals. They would then run over the mines, creating a duststorm which roared like thunder. Eyes would then see nothing. Ears would then see nothing.

And then the duststorm would settle and a blessed silence would cover the field. We could then see fragments of broken young bodies covering the plain: scraps of flesh and bones, some stuck to thorn bushes or pebbles. It was as if the sky had rained flesh and blood and pieces of broken bone on that field. . . .[25]

The corny sub-Hafizian language betrays the writer's state of mind. We are in the presence of that implacable nostalgia, that endless lamentation of the exile, which translates itself into violence just as soon as the world threatens to expose it as a fraud. The example set by the followers of Khomeini was soon projected around the world. Sunni Muslims, who believe on the authority of the Koran that suicide is categorically forbidden, have nevertheless been sucked into the Shi'ite maelstrom to become martyrs in the war against Satan. The cult of death seems to make sense of a world in which evil prevails; moreover it gives unprecedented power to the martyr, who no longer has anything to fear. The cult is both a protest against modern nihilism and a form of it—a last-ditch attempt to rescue Islam from the abyss of nothingness by showing that it can still demand the ultimate proof of devotion.

And the attempt seems to have succeeded. It is not too great an exaggeration to say that this new confluence of Sunni orthodoxy and Shi'ite extremism has laid the foundations for a worldwide Islamic revival. For the first time in centuries Islam appears, both in the eyes of its followers and in the eyes of the infidel, to be a single religious movement united around a single goal. Nor is it an exaggeration to suggest that one major factor in producing this unwonted unity is Western civilization and the process of globalization that it has set in motion. In the days when East was East and West was West, it was possible for Muslims to devote their lives to pious observances and to ignore the evil that prevailed in the *dar al-harb*. But when that evil spreads around the globe, cheerfully offering freedoms and permissions in place of the austere requirements of a religious code, so that the *dar al-islam* is invaded by it, old antagonisms are awakened, and with them the old need for allies against the infidel.

CHAPTER 4

GLOBALIZATION

IT IS THANKS to Western prosperity, Western legal systems, Western forms of banking, and Western communications that human initiatives now reach so easily across frontiers to affect the lives and aspirations of people all over the globe. However, as my argument has implied, Western civilization depends on an idea of citizenship that is not global at all, but rooted in territorial jurisdiction and national loyalty. By contrast, Islam, which has been until recently remote from the Western world and without the ability to project its message, is founded on an ideal of godliness which is entirely global in its significance, and which regards territorial jurisdiction and national loyalty as compromises with no intrinsic legitimacy of their own. Although there have been attempts to manufacture nationalisms both appropriate to the Islamic temperament and conducive to a legitimate political order, they have fragmented under the impact of sectarian or tribal allegiances, usually giving way to military dictatorship or one-man, one-family, or one-party tyranny. Islam itself

remains, in the hearts of those who live under these tyrannies, a permanent call to a higher life, and a reminder that
power and corruption will rule in this world until the reign
established by the Prophet is restored.

Terrorism has a long history in the Islamic countries,
being the usual recourse of those who reject the legitimacy
of the prevailing sovereign power. Until recently, however,
it modeled itself on the Assassins, and took powerful or
symbolic individuals as its targets. In nineteenth-century
Russia, terrorism took a new and more destructive form,
involving indiscriminate bombings and acts of destruction
which, according to one estimate, claimed 17,000 victims
between 1894 and 1917.[1] The Russian methods finally led
to a successful revolution, and have been adopted by the
postwar nationalist movements in Western Europe, notably by the IRA and ETA, as well as by the urban revolutionaries of the 1960s in Italy, France, and Germany, by the
PLO, and by the left-wing insurgents in Latin America.
Those groups have formed mutually supportive networks
for the exchange of training and expertise, and it is due to
the globalizing process that these networks are available
also to the Islamist extremists.

Nevertheless, Islamist terrorism is a distinct development in two ways. Islamism is not a nationalist movement,
still less a bid to establish a new kind of secular state. It
rejects the modern state and its secular law in the name of
a "brotherhood" that reaches secretly to all Muslim hearts,
uniting them against the infidel. And because its purpose

is religious rather than political, the goal is incapable of realization. The Muslim Brotherhood failed even to change the political order of Egypt, let alone to establish itself as a model of Koranic government throughout the Muslim world. Where Islamists succeed in gaining power—as in Iran, Sudan, and Afghanistan—the result is not the reign of peace and piety promised by the Prophet, but murder and persecution on a scale matched in our time only by the Nazis and the Communists.[2] The Islamist, like the Russian nihilist, is an exile in this world; and when he succeeds in obtaining power over his fellow human beings, it is in order to punish them for being human.

Globalization does not mean merely the expansion of communications, contacts, and trade around the globe. It means the transfer of social, economic, political, and juridical power to global organizations, by which I mean organizations that are located in no particular sovereign jurisdiction, and governed by no particular territorial law. The growth of such organizations is, in my view, a regrettable by-product of our addiction to freedom. Whether in the form of multinational corporations, international courts, or transnational legislatures, these organizations pose a new kind of threat to the only form of sovereignty that has brought lasting (albeit local) peace to our planet. And when terrorism too becomes globalized, the threat is amplified a hundred-fold

With al-Qaʿeda, therefore, we encounter the real impact of globalization on the Islamic revival.[3] To belong to this "base" is to accept no territory as home, and no human law as authoritative. It is to commit oneself to a state of permanent exile, while at the same time resolving to carry out God's work of punishment. But the techniques and infrastructure on which al-Qaʿeda depends are the gifts of the new global institutions. It is Wall Street and Zurich that produced the network of international finance that enables Osama bin Laden to conceal his wealth and to deploy it anywhere in the world. It is Western enterprise with its multinational outreach that produced the technology that bin Laden has exploited so effectively against us. And it is Western science that developed the weapons of mass destruction he would dearly like to obtain. His wealth, too, would be inconceivable without the vast oil revenues brought to Saudi Arabia from the West, there to precipitate the building boom from which his father profited. And this very building boom, fueled by a population explosion that is itself the result of global trade, is a symbol of the West and its outreach. The appearance of Arabia has been permanently altered by it—and altered, in the feelings of many Muslims, for the worse. Concrete high-rises dwarf the minarets, domestic alleyways give way to pretentious boulevards or jerry-built slums, and the hideous, unfriendly style of international modernism overlays and extinguishes the delicate fabric of the Muslim city.

It may seem quixotic to emphasize the role of architecture in the present conflict. But we should remember

Mohammed Atta's nostalgia for the old town of Aleppo and reflect on what has happened to the face of the Middle East under the impact of Western architectural norms, which have a symbolic significance at least equal to that of Western dress and Western manners. Architectural modernism was introduced with fanfares of globalist propaganda by the Bauhaus and by Le Corbusier, who envisaged their new style of architecture as both the symbol and the instrument of a radical break with the past. This architecture was conceived in the spirit of detachment from place and history and home. It was "the international style," a gesture against the nation-state and the homeland, an attempt to remake the surface of the earth as a single uniform habitat from which differences and boundaries would finally disappear.

In the West, where democratic procedures and legal norms give power to the citizen, the impact of international modernism has here and there been controlled and limited. Although the damage has been great, many cities retain their local character, and villages hold out against the tide. The great exception—Germany—remains committed to architectural modernism as a symbol and instrument of its cultural self-repudiation. And the modern German city can be seen as part of the long sad coda of Germany's defeat—the final transformation of a nation that does not dare to show its face without the benefit of plastic surgery. Elsewhere in Europe—notably in Italy, France, and Spain—the international style has been resisted; churches dominate the skyline and streets are still bordered by humane facades. A conscious effort has been made to retain the character of both town and country, in the knowledge that they define an experience of the home-land, and that the homeland is the thing to which the citizen's loyalty is owed.

Americans have been careless of their cities, with the result that no one wants to live in them. But their suburbs radiate homeliness and comfort, and the country itself lies somewhere out there along the interstate, a still wild, open frontier that belongs to all of us, and we to it. Against the odds America has retained the aspect and the atmosphere of home.

In the Middle East, however, where land is disposed of by the governing power, and planning regulations are either non-existent or ignored, the landscape and cityscape have been mutilated beyond recognition. It was Le Corbusier who showed the way. Having failed to persuade the French authorities to adopt his plan to bulldoze Paris north of the Seine and replace it with militarized towers of glass, Le Corbusier worked on successive French governments, in-cluding the Vichy regime, to implement his insolent plan to raze the old city of Algiers, capital of Algeria, which was then a French colony. He succeeded at last, and after the war the bulldozers moved in, with catastrophic results. Thanks to the enormous profits that accrue to the modern-ist ways of building, Le Corbusier became a hero of the architectural establishment, and his repulsive plan for this once beautiful city is now illustrated in all the standard Western textbooks of architecture.

Le Corbusier showed the European intelligentsia how the inferior people of North Africa should be treated: such, surely, was Atta's perception. Since Le Corbusier's time, the rush of speculative building—most of it illegal and on land that is officially "publicly owned," and fueled by the demographic explosion—has entirely transformed the visual aspect and daily rhythm of the Middle Eastern cities.[4] Whatever hope there might have been that people would come to define their loyalties in terms of territory rather than faith has been obliterated by the impact of Western technology, which seems to believe in neither. And if we wish to understand in full the resentment of Palestinians towards Israeli settlements on the West Bank, we should not neglect the visual damage that these settlements have caused, introducing modernist styles and materials, sweeping roadways, and ubiquitous light pollution into a landscape that had worn its biblical aspect for centuries, with star-spangled nights above stone-built villages and historic cities like Jenin.

As the examples of bin Laden, al-Qa'eda, and the September 11 terrorists demonstrate, Islamism is not a cry of distress from the "wretched of the earth." It is an implacable summons to war, issued by globetrotting middle-class Muslims, many of them extremely wealthy, and most of them sufficiently well versed in Western civilization and its benefits to be able to exploit the modern world to the full. These Muslims are products of the globalizing process, and Western civilization has so amplified their message that it travels with them around the world.

It may be hard to sympathize with these spoiled and self-indulgent advocates of violence. But it is not hard to sympathize with the feelings upon which they depend for their following. Globalization, in the eyes of its advocates, means free trade, increased prosperity, and the steady erosion of despotic regimes by the growing demand for freedom. In the eyes of its critics, however, it means the loss of sovereignty, together with large-scale social, economic, and aesthetic disruption. It also means an invasion of images that evoke outrage and disgust as much as envy in the hearts of those who are exposed to them. In the United States, where pornography is protected as free speech, people are able to accept that this assault on human dignity is the price we must pay for freedoms too precious to relinquish. But if you have not known those freedoms, and believe in any case that happiness resides not in freedom but in submission to God's law, the impact of pornography is devastating.[5] No less devastating, for pious Muslims, are what they see as the indecent clothes and behavior of young women in the West—clothes and behavior that are in no way modified when those women travel on business or as tourists to Muslim countries, there to presume on a toleration which they are willing to reciprocate but do little or nothing to earn.

People in the West live in a public space in which each person is surrounded and protected by his rights, and where all behavior that poses no obvious physical threat is permitted. But people in Muslim countries live in a space that is shared but private, where nobody is shielded by his rights from communal judgment, and where communal judgment is experienced as the judgment of God. Western habits, Western morals, Western art, music, and television are seen not as freedoms but as temptations. And the normal response to temptation is either to give in to it, or to punish those who offer it. Many Muslim *muhajiroun* do both. Like Atta, they drink, gamble, and fornicate in the flesh-pots of America, while secretly plotting revenge against the thing that made these indulgences possible.

Globalization, therefore, offers militant Islam the opportunity that it has lacked since the Ottoman retreat from central Europe. It both concentrates the resolve of the believer and offers him a sword with which to prosecute God's will. Muslim states do not have the loyalty of their people, who are not citizens but subjects, contemptuous (for the most part) of their rulers. Hence, Muslim *states* have not recently posed a threat to the West. If they seem to do so, it is only because they form the shield around some crazy tyrant, whose power reaches no further than his weapons. Globalization, however, has brought into being a true Islamic *umma*, which identifies itself across borders in terms of a global form of legitimacy, and which attaches itself like a parasite to global institutions and techniques that are the by-products of Western democracy. This new form of globalized Islam is undeniably threatening, since it satisfies a hunger for membership that globalization itself has created. It calls on the old nostalgia of the *muhajir*, and directs it not at some local usurper but at God's enemies, wherever they are.

THE PERSONAL STATE

Interestingly, however, the principal target of al-Qa'eda, as of the late Ayatollah Khomeini, is neither Western civilization, nor Christianity, nor global capitalism, nor anything else that can be given an abstract profile—it is the United States, conceived as a sovereign nation-state. In an uncanny way, the Islamists have identified the core component of the system that they wish to destroy. It is not the American people who are the enemy. It is the American state, conceived as an autonomous agent acting freely on the stage of international politics, and so calling on itself the wrath of God. When Khomeini described America as "the Great Satan" he meant it literally. And his doing so showed that he had grasped the fundamental difference between the West and the rest: namely, that in the West, but not in the rest, there is a political process generating corporate agency, collective responsibility, and moral personality in the state.

The point here may easily be overlooked by those who see politics in terms of movements, processes, forces, and power struggles, and who neglect the difference that has been made to all these things by the legacy of over two millennia of Roman law. Like a firm or a church, a nation-state is not merely a collection of individuals. It is a moral and legal person, which acts on its own behalf and is liable for what it does. The nation-state can therefore be praised and blamed, hated and loved, and the form of member-ship that it offers is also a bond of trust between indi-vidual citizens and the corporation in whose decision-mak-ing they share.

The very same political process that turns subjects into citizens turns the state into a collective expression of its citizens' way of life. When we speak of the United States as negotiating a treaty, as building up its army, as declaring war on terrorism, we are not speaking meta-phorically. These things are the genuine actions of a cor-porate person, in which all U.S. citizens are to some extent implicated, but which are the actions of no individual. When we speak in the same terms of Iraq or North Korea, however, we are speaking obliquely. There is no such en-tity as Iraq, only a legal fiction erected by the United Nations for the purpose of dealing with whichever indi-vidual, clique, or faction is for the moment holding the people of that country hostage. The form of corporate agency established by Western political systems has not been established elsewhere in the world. The states of the non-Western world are impersonal states, machines in their rulers' hands. They make no decisions, take no responsibility, and can be neither praised nor blamed, but exist merely as shields and weapons in the hands of those whose advantages they secure. This was made explicit under the Leninist system of communist government, which was founded on the theory of "parallel structures." Every office of the Soviet state was shadowed by an office of the "vanguard Party," which exercised all the power but was wholly unaccountable for doing so.

This too casts some light on September 11. The attacks were designed to wound the United States in its decision-making part. The Pentagon, the White House, and the World Trade Center represent the three principal spheres of political agency—military, governmental, and economic—and the three ways in which the United States makes itself felt around the globe. And they bear witness to the reality of the country as an autonomous agent that can make decisions on its own behalf and can call upon the loyalty of its citizens to adopt those decisions as their own. The attacks were assaults on the *person* of the United States, and therefore on each and every citizen of that country.

The difference between "the West and the rest" is captured in this idea of the corporate person—an idea that has its origins in Roman law and no real equivalent in the *fiqh*. The personal state is characterized by a constitution, by a rule of law, and by a rotation of office-holders. Its decisions are collectively arrived at by a process that may not be wholly democratic, but which nevertheless includes every citizen and provides the means whereby each citizen can adopt the outcome as his own. Personal states have an inherent preference for negotiation over compulsion, and for peace over war. They can live peacefully side-by-side despite disputed borders, as do the United States and Canada, while awaiting the outcome of a legal case that will settle the dispute. And they foster the growth of a national loyalty and a territorial jurisdiction in which the absolute demands of religion are tempered by the overarching need for toleration and common obedience to a secular power. The legitimacy of this power resides partly in custom, tradition, and the long-standing habits of the homeland; but it also depends upon the negotiated consent of the citizens who, through their participation in the political process, make the decisions of the state into decisions of their own.

Of course, that is a somewhat idealized picture of the modern nation-state. But it conveys the ideal to which Western states have aspired, and which has shaped their distinctive form of politics. Although democracy has been an immensely important component in the emerging nation-states of the modern world, it is more a consequence than a cause of their personality. In the absence of corporate personality, experiments in democratic government lead to social disruption, factionalism, and either the tyranny of the majority or the seizure of power by a clique. This we have witnessed time and again in Africa, and those who believe that the remedy for the "failed states" of the region is to introduce democratic elections fail to see that without the framework of institutions and the underlying territorial loyalty, democratization is merely a staging post on the way to tyranny.

The personal state is answerable to its citizens, and its decisions can be imputed to them not least because they, as citizens, participate in the political process. When it fights on their behalf it does not drag them into conflicts that are none of their business but involves them in conflicts of their own. In this it should be contrasted with the principal forms of government that prevail outside the "West": the one-party state, the religious state, individual tyranny, and the so-called "failed state," in which the apparatus of government has simply fallen into disuse, leaving the people unprotected against criminals, marauders, and terrorists, as they are now unprotected in many parts of South America. Although all these varieties of state are represented at the United Nations, and all are accorded there the status of persons in international law, none of them has full corporate personality as I have described it. For one thing, they all lack effective internal opposition. Often during the Cold War commentators wrote of a contest between "hawks" and "doves" in the Kremlin, or of opposition to communist policies in this or that professional or military grouping within the party. And similar things are said today about the Islamic Republic of Iran. The fact remains, however, that there is no defined role for opposition in those states, no way in which an opposing party can peacefully compete for power with the one that currently possesses it, and therefore no way in which opposition can be used to create a government based on dialogue. Decisions are made by an unanswerable minority and imposed willy-nilly on the country. The role of opposition, which is to make government accountable to the people, remains unfulfilled.

Any conflict with a non-personal state is therefore a conflict with some faction or individual within it. There cannot be victory in such a conflict unless the faction or individual is destroyed. This we have already experienced in the Gulf War. The Iraqi soldiers who had occupied Kuwait were quickly driven from their positions—after all, it was not their war, and not one of them had the slightest desire to lay down his life for Saddam Hussein. They were helpless conscripts in the schemes of a dictator. But because the allies did nothing to depose Saddam Hussein, the seeming victory was not a victory at all, but merely a restoration of the status quo ante and a renewal of Saddam's implacable enmity. The formal defeat of Iraq was the defeat of a legal fiction. The real victory was that of Saddam, who retained control over his subjects in the face of an alliance of nation-states that proved powerless to unseat him.

The asymmetry between personal states and the impersonal forces that now confront them can be witnessed in the case of Israel. The British protectorate of Palestine, carved out of the defunct Ottoman Empire, was opened to large-scale Jewish immigration by the Balfour Declaration of 1917. Later, in the wake of the Holocaust, the desire of Jews for a state of their own became irresistible, and the retreat of the British from their protectorate was hastened by the terrorist methods of the Stern Gang. Israel quickly transformed itself thereafter into a nation-state by allying a historical national identity with an existing territorial jurisdiction. The Jews' pre-existing attachment to the Promised Land endowed the rule of law that the British had begun to establish in Palestine with the much-needed territorial loyalty. The result is that the state of Israel exhibits personal sovereignty on the Western model, and a genuinely democratic system of government. Few people doubt the injustice done to the Palestinian Arabs, both Muslim and Christian, in this process. But the fact remains that, for better or worse, Israel now exists in the heart of the Middle East, a personal nation-state surrounded, since the virtual annexation of Lebanon by Syria, by tyrannies, factional groupings, and terrorist movements that have only a fictitious personality either in fact or in law.

There is as yet no Palestinian state, nor was there ever, strictly speaking, a Palestinian nation, over and above the collection of historic creed communities that coexisted in the Holy Land under a succession of imperial rules—most recently Ottoman and British. The nominal leader of the Palestinians—Yassir 'Arafat—has never been elected by them, but was projected into eminence by the PLO, itself a terrorist organization on the model of the IRA, with a global network devoted to a local cause.[6] By astute diplomacy on the world stage 'Arafat has won recognition for that cause; but he has neither the authority to pursue accommodation with Israel, nor the power to lead the Palestinians in an all-out war. Nor can he control the terrorist organizations that reside under his aegis and draw on the support of Islamic militants throughout the world.

Organizations like Hamas and the Islamic Jihad take their inspiration from the Muslim Brotherhood and the Hizbullah. They do not work through diplomacy or negotiation, but through violence, and suicide bombings are now their principal device. In these circumstances it is almost impossible for Israel to form a coherent policy towards the Palestinians. To destroy 'Arafat is pointless, if it leads to no change in the suicide attacks. To negotiate with him is also pointless, since he does not represent the people on whose behalf he claims to speak. In the absence of a corporate person with which the Palestinians as a whole can identify, and whose decisions they can make their own, all negotiation is futile, and all force unfocused.

In the face of this, the argument for a Palestinian state is surely overwhelming. However it is doubtful that a Palestinian state, if founded, would easily develop the kind of corporate personality that I have attributed to the United States. For this would require, if my argument is right, the emergence of territorial loyalties that transcend the bonds of religion and *'asabiya* and express themselves through some participatory form of citizenship. It would require, in other words, the same kind of radical break with local history that we see in Israel.

Israel, meanwhile, suffers all the agonies of a personal state at war. It takes collective responsibility for its aggressive gestures, and its politicians rise and fall in response to the constant internal dialogue over principles and policies. Its leaders are subjected to criticism both at home and abroad, and, in its efforts to maintain the freedoms and rights that are the hallmark of personal government, Israel exposes itself to a constant stream of atrocities. The world supposes that Israel is at war with the Palestinians: but the Palestinians do not exist as a genuine agent in this war, and besides it is only in Israel that any Palestinian Arab can cast his vote in an election and expect to have some influence on what is done. To say this is not to approve of Israel's current policy towards the West Bank. Nor is it a reason to deny the plight of the Palestinians. It is simply to indicate the structural difficulty of the problem, and the near impossibility of making peace when there is no accountable agent with whom to negotiate.

If we see the Palestinian conflict in this way, we shall be led to reject the currently fashionable view that the terrorist threat to America comes from America's support for Israel. On the contrary. It is Israel's relation to America that makes *Israel* the target of militant Islam. The Palestinians have a legitimate grievance. But the Muslim states of the Middle East have done little or nothing to support them in this grievance. Instead they have exploited it for their own imperial ends, like the Syrians and the Iranians in Lebanon, or Saddam Hussein in Kuwait. When Israel became the target for the Islamic militants of Hizbullah it was not in order to achieve some settlement favorable to the Palestinian people. It was in order to punish Israel as an outreach of the West in the *dar al-islam*. The Islamic militants can therefore be satisfied with nothing short of the total destruction of Israel. For Israel is a nation-state established where no nation-state should be—a place where the only law should be the *shari'a*, and the only loyalty that of Islam. Meanwhile, the occupation of the West Bank, proceeding as it does not through administration but through modernist architecture, is a vivid symbol of the globalizing process: it exhibits a will to permanent and irreversible change, by which local identities are razed and the earth re-shaped as an ubiquitous nowhere.

The problem posed by conflict when one of the parties has no real corporate personality is not confined to the Middle East. Globalization is spreading it to the West, and the terrorist attacks are our first large-scale encounter with it. Furthermore, they bring home to us the fact that the remedies devised for dealing with global problems are ineffective against the new kinds of agency that globalization has created. International law can do nothing to control al-Qa'eda, nor is the United Nations effective against organizations that neither are, nor aspire to be, nation-states. While it is possible to bring pressure to bear on individual states that harbor terrorists, this pressure is ineffective against a failed state, or against a state like Iran, which is happy to ignore requests from Satan.

TRANSNATIONAL GOVERNMENT

But there is another and, in a way, more serious aspect of globalization. It has been a ruling principle of Western politics that every extension of human powers should be accompanied by an extension of the law, as a means of controlling those powers and ensuring that they are not abused. Inevitably, therefore, as the global impact of human decisions increases, so does the demand for new legislative bodies with which to control that impact and direct it to the common good. Until recently this kind of legal control was exerted through international law, backed by treaties, of which the charter forming the United Nations was the most important. It was assumed that sovereignty remained with the individual states, and that the benefits from international law were such that they would willingly uphold its judgments, lest they be excluded from the club. As originally conceived, therefore, the United Nations was exactly that—a union of nations, each of which could one day be constituted as a nation-state, and each of which meanwhile enjoyed the legal personality bestowed upon it by international law.

Many commentators still believe that the UN is the benign institution that its founders intended it to be, and that the problems of the modern world arise largely because powerful countries like the United States prefer to settle their disputes directly, on terms more favorable to themselves than could be obtained from the court of international opinion. It seems to me, however, that this optimistic view is no longer sustainable. For it ignores the fact that, with the exception of delegates from personal states, those who turn up to UN meetings literally have no business being there. They are not the representatives of the people from whose territory they come, and if they speak for anyone it is for the party, faction, or tyrant who sent them. Moreover, as Rosemary Righter has shown, the UN and its subordinate institutions are wholly prey to corruption, consuming vast resources by the relentless extension of unaccountable bureaucratic power.[7] These institutions are less means of resolving disputes than means of creating them, by dressing up the crimes of unaccountable tyrants as though they were the corporate decisions of nation-states.

Matters have significantly worsened in recent decades, as new forms of transnational legislation threaten the sovereignty and the aspirations of the smaller countries of the world. It would be a coherent response to globalization to encourage the emergence of nation-states in all places where there is an embryonic territorial jurisdiction. In this way each nation could make its own choices for the future, and avoid being swept away by the global tide. And with the emergence of territorial jurisdictions and genuinely accountable governments, the terrorist threat would almost certainly dwindle, as people learn to attach their loyalties to real fragments of earth rather than imaginary vistas of heaven and thereby to see human life for what it is—namely, a process of accommodation with one's neighbors. But this is not what is happening. The embryonic states of Africa and Asia, for example, are subject to WTO regulations that will unavoidably ruin their local food economies by forcing them to compete on equal terms with massively subsidized industrial food producers in the West. Genetically modified crops, whose seeds are patented by Western multinationals, will very probably drive the old crops from the market, compelling third-world farmers, through the system of Trade Related Intellectual Property Rights, to buy their seeds in the West. In other words, the agrarian economies of Africa will be expropriated by transnational legislation that their people are powerless to annul.

I mention the WTO because it is so widely perceived as an instrument of "Western imperialism," and not only by those Westerners who fly around the world to demonstrate against its meetings. In fact, almost every international institution, however good its intentions, is attempting to pass laws, conventions, and treaties—if only to justify its existence and to have something for its overpaid bureaucrats to do.[8] Repeated protests against the decisions of global summits go unheeded, and a constant stream of unaccountable regulations issues from the meetings of the Western powers as though the rest had no choice but to accept them.

The global financial institutions have acquired comparable sovereign powers. The World Bank and the IMF, though founded with the purpose of securing global financial stability, are now widely perceived as instruments of Western domination. After all, they deal in dollars, and the money that they give or lend can be spent only in an economy dominated by Western technology and Western exports. By accepting this money a state is dragged unavoidably into the global maelstrom.[9] Moreover, being compelled in the nature of things to negotiate with governments, the World Bank and the IMF subsidize the tyrants and gangsters who have expropriated the political life of the countries where they have come to power. Nor is there any real pressure on such transnational institutions to account for their actions. A large number of the enormous IMF loans made in recent years to the states of the former Soviet Union have disappeared into the same Swiss bank accounts that have been used to milk the Soviet people for fifty years. This has led to a few vaguely reproachful noises, but to no penalties corresponding to the enormity of the crime.

To some extent the United States has remained unaffected by this growth in transnational legislation. Its presidents have been reluctant to sign any treaty not clearly in the nation's interest, and they react adversely to any proposals that would diminish United States sovereignty or the ability of the country to defend its territory. But, the critics say, this is because the United States is able to dominate the crucial bodies, and to ensure that regulations—

such as those issued by the WTO—operate always in its national interest.

A telling example is the proposed treaty to establish an International Criminal Court—a pie-eyed dream of Western liberals, designed to replace wars by judicial processes, and to charge belligerents with war crimes. It seems clear that the Senate will not ratify this treaty even though President Clinton reluctantly added his signature to it. For the treaty will curtail the freedoms to make sound military judgments and to make pre-emptive strikes against a potential enemy. Hence, it will violate national sovereignty in an area where sovereignty is the pre-condition of survival. The court will be appointed by no accountable government, and its judges will include many from impersonal states, who will act simply as tools in the hands of unscrupulous factions or dictators. It is surely a welcome development that the United States is rebelling against this particular piece of transnational legislation. But it has yet to wake up to the principle that almost all transnational legislation is a threat to *someone's* sovereignty.

Pertinent in the present context is the UN Convention on Refugees and Asylum, ratified in 1951, at a time when migration was not common and asylum rarely offered or sought. This piece of legislation obliges our governments to offer asylum to all who need it, and to give hospitality meanwhile to those who claim it. As a result of global mobility, some two million people arrive every year in Europe, ostensibly seeking asylum but in fact wishing to profit from the black economy, and in any case enjoying the obligatory hospitality required by the UN Convention. As a result, European states have lost conrol of their borders, have unknown numbers of illegal residents, and have black economies that grow larger by the week. Moreover, anyone who suggests that the UN Convention is anachronistic, politically dangerous, and socially destructive is subjected to intimidating criticism and risks being denounced as a "racist" or worse.

The political and economic advantages that lead people to seek asylum in the West are the result of territorial jurisdiction. Yet territorial jurisdictions can survive only if borders are controlled. Transnational legislation, acting together with the culture of repudiation, is therefore rapidly undermining the conditions that make Western freedoms durable. The effect of this on the politics of France and Holland is now evident to everyone. And when we find among the "asylum seekers" the vast majority of those Islamist cells that have grown up in London, Paris, and Hamburg, we begin to recognize just how much the political culture of the West is bent on a path of self-destruction.

THE NEW IMPERIUM

But this brings us to a deeper question: is the nation-state a durable arrangement? Consider England—the most successful example of a localized territorial jurisdiction in the modern world. Just when and for how long did it exist as a nation-state? The skeptic would say: for about the length of time required to absorb its northern neighbor; in other words, from the Glorious Revolution of 1688 to the Act of Union with Scotland of 1707. Thereafter it expanded relentlessly into an empire, acquired, in Sir John Seeley's famous words, "in a fit of absence of mind"[10] —i.e., not by policy, still less by any corporate decision on the nation's behalf, but by "an invisible hand," in other words, as the unintended by-product of a myriad actions, very few of which were actions of the state. And those who accuse the United States of being, or becoming, a new imperial power are pointing to a similar process, whereby the legislative powers of smaller states are being steadily expropriated by transnational institutions that only the United States can really control or escape from.

Perhaps the most telling example of the invisible hand of imperialism, however, is not the United States, but the European Union (EU). Europe is the home of the nation-state, and the crucible in which the idea of secular and territorial jurisdiction first took shape. At the same time recent history has implanted in many of the European elites a skepticism towards the national idea and a desire for a transnational federation in place of it. The British and Scandinavian people are reluctant to accept this; the Mediterranean people accept it only because they do not take it wholly seriously. But many of the French and the Germans remain wedded to the idea as the best way of maintaining the peace and prosperity of Europe. At the same time, the majority of the decisions that are forcing the Europeans to abandon their national sovereignties are made by people who have no intention to produce an imperial power.

Nevertheless, despite the fact that virtually nobody explicitly wants it, a process is under way that will effectively extinguish the national democracies of Europe and erect in their place a European superstate, nominally a democracy but with largely unaccountable legislative powers, hidden in bureaucratic institutions with their own long-term agendas. Already most laws passed by the United Kingdom Parliament are imposed by *diktaat* from the Brussells bureaucracy, and the few areas of legislative competence that remain are being steadily eroded by revisions to the Treaty of Rome. Scotland and Wales are still present on the official maps of Europe. But the nation-state that did most to create the modern world—namely England—has already been replaced by "regions" that have no historical meaning and defy all the local loyalties to which English patriotism responds.

There are those who regret this, and those who welcome it, as an opportunity to revive the idea of Western civilization on the continent where that civilization was born. The question that we need to ask, however, is whether this new form of imperial government can really answer to the problems that now confront us. If my argument in this book is correct, the European superstate will not be held in place by its political institutions. Only in the context of a pre-political loyalty will those institutions have legitimacy in the eyes of the citizens, and it is precisely the absence of a pan-European loyalty that gave rise to the federal project in the first place.

Suppose a village has existed for centuries as an autonomous community, its residents making decisions collectively through their elected council and enjoying all the benefits and burdens of self-government. And suppose that a neighboring, similarly self-governing but somewhat larger, town proposes to amalgamate with the village, arguing that the increased prospects for trade and commerce fully justify the move, and that the new community will be just as democratic and self-governing as the old ones. Suppose, finally, that the villagers are persuaded, and do indeed enjoy the promised commercial benefits. They will find themselves as a result in a minority whenever a decision affecting their interests is to be made, and will be overridden by the town whenever the interests of town and village conflict. The new waste-disposal site will be placed on the borders of the village, not the town; the highway will be built through the village, not the town; and so on. In short, the villagers will experience their new democratic regime as a loss of sovereignty and a diminution in their democratic powers.

That is what is beginning to happen in Europe; indeed it has already happened with such measures as the expropriation of British fisheries by France and Spain and the imposition on Britain of metric weights and measures.

Americans do not need reminding, in this context, of the controversy over "states' rights." The evident conclusion is that, just as the village in my example will begin to resent the town and regard its decisions as illegitimate, so will the nation-states of Europe seek to break away from the Union, as the conflicts of interest re-animate the desire for national autonomy.

It is significant that, in all major crises that affect the root sentiments of the people, the national governments of Europe entirely set aside the transnational project to which they profess to be committed. After September 11 the British Prime Minister immediately joined with the United States, not only in condemning terrorism, but in committing his country and its armed forces to the fight against it. Other European countries made vague noises in the same direction, but did nothing. And subsequent pronouncements from France, Italy, and Germany have displayed a veiled but growing anti-Americanism, and a wish not to be involved. The French in particular prefer to see September 11 as an alien event affecting an alien people. A book arguing that no plane crashed into the Pentagon on September 11 and that those which hit the twin towers were guided there by the CIA has even become a bestseller in France.[11]

Similarly the French have refused to police the entrance to the channel tunnel, knowing that the best way to rid themselves of illegal immigrants is by passing them on to Britain, where the welfare deal is more attractive. In this matter that affects the national interest and national identity of the two countries, pre-political loyalty shows itself at once, and it is the very same loyalty that shaped Europe as a system of nation-states.

Nor is it likely that a new kind of pre-political loyalty could arise from the European Union. All the factors that formed the loyalties of the European peoples—shared language, shared religion, shared customs, shared legal systems, and shared ways of life—are absent. Hence, the European Union is rapidly destroying the territorial jurisdictions and national loyalties that have, since the Enlightenment, formed the basis of European legitimacy, while putting no new form of membership in their place. It is significant that separatist and nationalist movements, far from being eroded by the project of union, have grown under its aegis, taking heart from the EU's antipathy to existing nationalisms to promote rival nationalisms of their own. Hence the renewed activities of the IRA and the Basque separatist organization ETA.

On the other hand, the very fervor with which the project of union is promoted by the European elites is some indication that the national loyalties of Europe are in decline. The EU is a political expression of the culture of repudiation that I described in chapter 2, and goes hand-in-hand with legislative initiatives from the European Commission and the European courts that could be used to bind the entire continent in a regime of enforced political correctness. The commission proposes a Europe-wide police force, with power to extradite from any jurisdiction to any other within the Union, and with a list of extraditable offenses that include "racism and xenophobia." This offense is unrecognized in English law and as yet undefined by the courts. But anybody who has followed the reasoning of the European elites knows how it could be used: namely, to suppress any kind of nationalist opposition to the centralized bureaucracy.

Entering this new and bewildering political labyrinth the Muslim immigrant will certainly find a freedom and a prosperity that are unfamiliar in his country of origin. He will also enjoy welfare benefits, free education—or at any rate "education"—for his children, and free medical services. He will find plenty of work on the illegal market, since the states of the European Union have raised the cost of employing people to the point where small enterprises can no longer afford to offer work in the official economy. What the Muslim immigrant will not find, however, is any process of nation-building that might serve to recruit him to membership in the surrounding social order. He will live in strict isolation, and regard the world in which he earns his living as of no independent concern to him. Such membership as he enjoys will come to him from his family and the immigrant community to which his family belongs. And it will depend upon their shared obedience to the rituals of prayer and fasting and to the revealed will of God.

The new European superstate therefore offers a

breeding ground for Islamic terrorists. Just as the official culture of Europe involves a repudiation of the nation and its pride, so does the Muslim terrorist target the nation-state as the true work of Satan. The attacks on America were a response to the world's most successful attempt at nation-building, which projects its power, its freedom, and its detritus so effectively around the globe. All the principal actors in the atrocities of September 11 had resided in Europe, and received there both training and indoctrination through the local cells of al-Qaʻeda. The plot to attack America was not hatched in any Muslim country, but on the continent where the West began.

CHAPTER 5

CONCLUSION

MANY TERRORISTS are nihilists, who wish to vent their disappointment by destroying the sham society by which they are surrounded. Such were the terrorists so brilliantly portrayed by Turgenev and Conrad, and whose murderous campaigns have been described by Anna Geifman.[1] But nihilism is the other side of religion: it is the disappointed howl of the believer on discovering that God is dead. The true nihilist is incapable of settling for the world of compromise, toleration, and secular loyalties that the rest of us enjoy, since it is a world deprived of absolutes. The death of God leaves only one remaining absolute, which is Nothingness. The duty to annihilate is the last remaining glimpse of the transcendental in the heart of the one who has lost all belief in it and who cannot live with the loss. The "death-intoxicated" character of the Russian nihilists, and of the revolutionaries who trod in their footsteps, is therefore of a piece with the "God-intoxicated" frenzy of the Shi'ite martyr.

Globalization has plunged the Islamic world into crisis by offering the spectacle of a secular society maintained eing by man-made laws, and achieving equilibrium without the aid of God. It has also obliterated many of the customs and ways of life of the Muslim people, extinguishing ancient pastoral traditions and replacing them with a phony and humiliating economy of pure consumption, fed not by labor but by oil. At the same time it has re-awakened the age-old nostalgia for a reign of goodness, in which those who corrupted the Prophet's community will be finally destroyed, and the true order of the *shari'a* established on earth. The resulting psychological mixture is explosive, and is bound to prompt young Muslims to express their discontent with the regimes that govern them, with the global economy that finances those regimes, and with the impious way of life that is intruding everywhere into the *dar al-islam*.

In the Muslim territories themselves, however, possibilities for organized political action are limited or non-existent. Only in the West, thanks to political freedoms that are the gift of a long tradition of political experiment and Christian self-denial, can opposition to the corrupt regimes that govern the *dar al-islam* be mounted. Almost all the plots of the Islamist terrorists—from the Shi'ite revolution in Iran to the September 11 attacks—have been hatched in the West by *muhajiroun* who live, frequently enjoying the protection of asylum, in seemingly harmless symbiosis with the settled communities that surround them. But, because no bond of membership can possibly join them to those communities, they fail to acquire the national loyalty of their hosts. Nor is any effort now made to integrate them or to offer such a national loyalty to their children. Unable either to organize opposition in their country of origin, or to join the society in which they live, they are therefore drawn to religious violence as the only proof of their identity. This alone enables them to rediscover the absolutes that they need, and to generate a form of membership and an *'asabiya* untainted by the *dar al-harb*.

In the face of this we in the West must, I believe, do what we can to reinforce the nation-state, which has brought the great benefits that distinguish the West from the rest, including the benefits of personal government, citizenship under a territorial jurisdiction, and government answerable to the people. This means that we must constrain the process of globalization, so as to neutralize its perceived image as a threat from the West to the rest. To act responsibly means revisiting many of our prejudices. All of the following have contributed to the present danger, and all need to be subjected to a re-examination:

• Our failure to adjust immigration policies to the goal of integration, and the reciprocal assumption that we should be free to travel anywhere around the globe, without first learning about the taboos and aspirations of the places that we visit.

• Our acceptance of "multiculturalism" as an educational and political goal, and our habit of denigrating the real national and political culture upon which we depend.

- Our corresponding commitment to "free trade," conceived as the WTO conceives it, namely, as a way of compelling other countries to remove the barriers that they have erected in defense of perceived local interest.

- Our easy acceptance of the multinational corporation as a legitimate legal person, even though it is subject to no particular sovereign jurisdiction and is able to own property in every part of the globe.

- Our seeming indifference as the authority of the secular law and territorial jurisdiction is eroded by predatory litigation at home, and by bureaucratic legislation from elsewhere.

- Our devotion to prosperity, and the habits of consumption that have led us to depend upon raw materials, such as oil, which cannot be obtained within our territory.

These habits, beliefs, and prejudices are deeply ingrained in the Western political process, and to question them will be hard. Nor can we expect a sudden reversal, since they are the unintended by-products of the Western political system. The "litigation explosion" is a telling instance of this fact. The citizen sees the law as his friend, the shield against those who would exploit or control him. But, seeing it in this way, he discovers another use for it: as a device for diverting resources to himself. The law then becomes a weapon not only in his own hands, but in the hands of his competitor. No citizen is protected by the law in America today, since it could be used by anyone against him in order to rob him of all that he has. This transformation of the law from friend to foe, and from equilibrating to disequilibrating device, was intended by no one, but arose like the British Empire, "in a fit of absence of mind."

Similarly with the other habits I have emphasized. They are unintended consequences of free association and secular law. We cannot reverse them overnight, or suppress the instincts that bring them into being. When people enjoy the benefits of citizenship they treat the world in an open and enterprising way; they become careless of the sacrifices on which sovereignty depends, and oblivious of the corrosive force of human contact. And this state of mind, which seems like good-natured toleration in the one who has succumbed to it, may be seen from outside as intolerable *hubris*, calling down judgment from the gods.

Nevertheless, we are rational creatures, and nothing prevents us from thinking through alternatives to the habits that have placed us in so much danger. Unless we are prepared to do so, the idea of a "war against terrorism" makes little sense. Terrorism is not, after all, an enemy, but a method used by the enemy. The enemy is of two kinds: the tyrant dictator, and the religious fanatic whom the tyrant protects. To act against the first is feasible, if we are prepared to play by the tyrant's rules. But to act against the second requires a credible alternative to the absolutes with which he conjures. It requires us not merely to believe in something, but to study how to put our beliefs into practice.

NOTES

PREFACE

1. Samuel Huntington, *The Clash of Civilizations and the Remaking of World Order* (New York: Simon & Schuster, 1996). Huntington's thesis was first put forward in an article published in *Foreign Affairs* in 1993.

2. In this book I transliterate Arabic words only imperfectly, making no distinction between the various consonants that resemble "h" and "s," or between the long and short forms of the vowels "a" and "i." Masculine nouns in Arabic tend to have irregular plurals, and where necessary I have tried to indicate this. I give the standard notation ' for the guttural *'ain*, and ' for the glottal stop or *hamza*.

1. THE SOCIAL CONTRACT

1. Marcel Gauchet, *Le désenchantement du monde: une histoire politique de la religion* (Paris: Gallimard, 1985), published in English as *The Disenchantment of the World: A Political History of Religion,* trans. Oscar Burge (Princeton, N.J.: Princeton University Press, 1997).

2. See George H. Sabine and Thomas L. Thorson, *A History of*

Political Theory, 4th rev. ed. (Hinsdale, Ill.: Dryden Press, 1973), pp. 182-191.

3. The theory of the church as corporate person is given for the non-conformist churches by J. N. Figgis, *Churches in the Modern State,* 2nd ed. (London: Longmans, Green and Co., 1914), and for the Roman Catholic Church by Henri de Lubac, S.J., in *Catholicism: A Study of Dogma in Relation to the Corporate Destiny of Mankind* (London: Longmans, Green and Co.,1950).

4. *Leviathan*, pt. 2, ch. 21.

5. John Rawls, *A Theory of Justice*, Oxford 1972.

6. *The Decline of the West*, vol. 2, discussed in the U.S. edition of my *Philosopher on Dover Beach: Essays* (South Bend, Ind.: St. Augustine's Press, 1998), ch. 2.

7. The Urdu word *mullah* has entered the language via the British Empire in India. Like *imam* and *'alim*, it denotes no formal office but a self-generated holiness and religious knowledge, sufficient to entitle the one who possesses them to lead the community in prayer.

8. This point was stated explicitly by the thirteenth-century judge Henry de Bracton in his *De legibus et consuetudinibus Angliae* (Of the Laws and Customs of England), c. 1220, revised c. 1250.

9. Sir Henry Maine, in *Ancient Law: Its Connection with the Early History of Society and its Relation to Modern Ideas* (London: J. Murray, 1861), famously theorized the rise of modernity in terms of the transition from status to contract.

10. *England: An Elegy* (London: Chatto & Windus, 2000).

11. For an illuminating discussion of the post-Ottoman codes

as envisaged by those who first devised them, see Norman Anderson, *Law Reform in the Muslim World* (London: Athlone Press, 1976).

12. See the penetrating analysis by Elie Kedourie, *Politics in the Middle East* (Oxford: Oxford University Press, 1992).

13. David Fromkin, *A Peace to End All Peace: The Fall of the Ottoman Empire and the Creation of the Modern Middle East* (New York: Avon Books, 1990).

14. See the discussion of Aflaq in Hisham Sharabi, *Nationalism and Revolution in the Arab World* (Princeton, N.J.: Van Nostrand, 1966).

15. See René Girard, *Le bouc émissaire* (Paris: B. Grasset, 1982).

16. In an interview with *Le Monde* on November 5, 2001, Girard applied his theory to the events of September 11, arguing that the terrorists were animated by "mimetic rivalry" on a planetary scale. The attacks could only be understood, therefore, in religious terms.

2. ENLIGHTENMENT, CITIZENSHIP, AND LOYALTY

1. I have argued this point in "Man's Second Disobedience," in *The Philosopher on Dover Beach*.

2. J. E. E. Dalberg-Acton, Lord Acton, "Nationality," in *The History of Freedom and Other Essays*, ed. J. N. Figgis and R. V. Lawrence (London: Macmillan, 1907).

3. Benedict Anderson, *Imagined Communities: Reflections on the Origin and Spread of Nationalism* (London: Verso, 1982; 2nd ed., 1991).

4. J. G. Herder, *Outlines of a Philosophy of the History of Man*, trans. T. O. Churchill, 2nd ed., 2 vols. (London: L. Hansard, 1803) gives Herder's diffuse account of culture, as something distinct from and more fundamental than civilization: culture binds us, civilization loosens the chains. J. G. Fichte's *Addresses to the German Nation* of 1807–8 were a call to the Germans to come together as a nation, in the wake of Napoleon's conquest.

5. Edmund Burke in *Reflections on the Revolution in France* and Alexis de Tocqueville in *Democracy in America*.

6. I have defended these claims in *England: An Elegy*, ch. 6.

7. The issues raised by this sentence are so complex that it might be thought presumptuous to state the point so simply and laconically. However, life is short, and I urge the skeptical reader to study the concept of the *dhimmi* in Muslim law and jurisdiction. See Antoine Fattal, *Le Statut légal des non-musulmans en pays d'Islam* (Beirut: Impr. catholique, 1958). I have dealt with this question at some length, and in the context of the Lebanese conflict, in *A Land Held Hostage: Lebanon and the West* (London: Claridge Press, 1987).

8. Thucydides, "The Funeral Oration of Pericles," in *History of the Peleponnesian War*, bk. 2, ch. 40.

9. See James Madison, *The Federalist,* no. 10, in George W. Carey and James McClellan, eds., *The Federalist* (Dubuque, Iowa: Kendall/Hunt, 1990), pp. 46–49.

10. Alexis de Tocqueville, *Democracy in America;* John Stuart Mill, *Of Representative Government.*

11. Victor Davis Hanson, *The Western Way of War: Infantry Battle in Classical Greece* (New York: Knopf, 1989) and

Carnage and Culture: Landmark Battles in the Rise of West-ern Power (New York: Doubleday, 2001).

12. This qualified nationalism needs an extended defense, and in terms other than those adumbrated in this book. I have given the defense in two essays: "In Defence of the Nation," in *The Philosopher on Dover Beach,* and in "The First-person Plural," in Claudio Veliz, ed., *The Worth of Nations* (Boston: Boston University Press, 1993).

13. Burke, *Reflections on the Revolution in France.*

14. Americans should not assume that Islamist cells in the West are located only in Europe. See Steven Emerson, *American Jihad: The Terrorists Living among Us* (New York: Free Press, 2002).

15. See Walter K. Olson, *The Litigation Explosion: What Hap-pened When America Unleashed the Lawsuit* (New York: Truman Talley Books-Dutton, 1991).

16. Michael Polanyi, *Personal Knowledge: Towards a Post-critical Philosophy* (London: Routledge, 1958), pp. 231–35.

17. I have tried to present the case against Foucault and Derrida in *An Intelligent Person's Guide to Modern Culture* (South Bend, Ind.: St. Augustine's Press, 2000).

18. Edward Said, *Orientalism* (New York: Pantheon, 1978).

19. Robert Bly, *The Sibling Society* (London: Persus, 1996).

20. See my account of youth culture in *An Intelligent Person's Guide to Modern Culture.*

3. HOLY LAW

1. See Albert Hourani, *Arabic Thought in the Liberal Age: 1798–1939* (Oxford: Oxford University Press, 1962).

2. See, for example, the outstanding study by Malise Ruthven, *Islam in the World* (Harmondsworth: Penguin, 1984; new ed., Harmondsworth, 2000); the review of modern Islamic politics by Edward Mortimer, *Faith and Power: The Politics of Islam* (London: Faber and Faber, 1982); and the scholarly account by Bernard Lewis, *The Political Language of Islam* (Chicago: University of Chicago Press, 1988).

3. The most accessible survey of the classical sources remains that of Erwin I. J. Rosenthal, *Political Thought in Medieval Islam: An Introductory Outline* (Cambridge: Cambridge University Press, 1958).

4. Quoted in Rosenthal, *Political Thought in Medieval Islam,* p. 131.

5. *Ibid.,* p. 155.

6. See, for example, Nabil Saleh, *Unlawful Gain and Legitimate Profit in Islamic Law*: Riba, gharar *and Islamic Banking* (Cambridge: Cambridge University Press, 1986).

7. Ruthven, *Islam in the World,* p. 99.

8. See the summary in Rosenthal, *Political Thought in Medieval Islam,* pp. 94–102.

9. *Max Weber on Charisma and Institution Building: Selected Papers,* ed. S. N. Eisenstadt (Chicago: University of Chicago Press, 1968).

10. Spinoza, *Tractatus Politicus.*

11. Ruthven, *Islam in the World,* p. 178.

12. *Ibid.*

13. G. von Grunebaum, quoted in Ruthven, *Islam in the World,* p. 178; *mal* = hoard or store and the *mal Allah* is the traditional name for the public purse.

14. See Fattal, *Le Statut légal des non-musulmans en pays d'Islam.*

15. See Michael Mehaffy and Nikos Salingaros, "The End of the Modern World," openDemocracy.net, for January 2002. Aleppo, whose Arabic name, Halab, means "milk," is still one of the most vital and best preserved of Middle Eastern cities, with a Levantine mix of sects, a thriving Christian quarter, a maze of old streets, and many beautiful Ottoman houses—although the city sustained considerable damage during Hafiz el-Asad's exterminatory attack on the indigenous cadre of the Muslim Brotherhood in 1982. See the description in Shusha Guppy, *Three Journeys in the Levant* (London: Starhaven, 2001), pp. 65 *ff.*

16. On the rituals and the prayers of orthodox Sunni Islam, see Maurice Gaudefroy-Demombynes's classic account in *Muslim Institutions,* trans. John P. MacGregor (London: Allen & Unwin, 1950).

17. Since law derives from God and not the ruler, enforcement poses a complex problem for the Muslim. See Michael Cook's exemplary work of scholarship, *Commanding Right and Forbidding Wrong in Islamic Thought* (Cambridge: Cambridge University Press, 2001).

18. The distinction between common culture and high culture is drawn more precisely in my *Intelligent Person's Guide to Modern Culture.*

19. See the thorough account by Peter L. Bergen, *Holy War Inc: Inside the Secret World of Osama bin Laden* (London: Weidenfeld, 2001).

20. Burke, *Reflections on the Revolution in France.*

21. See Daniel Pipes, "Islam and Islamism: Faith and Ideol-

ogy," in *The National Interest* no. 59, Spring 2000.

22. See Leonard Binder, *Islamic Liberalism: A Critique of Development Ideologies* (Chicago: University of Chicago Press, 1988).

23. Quoted in Amir Taheri, *Holy Terror: Inside the World of Islamic Terrorism* (London: Sphere, 1987), p. 113.

24. The ritual cry of mourning *Ya Hussein! Ja Hussein!*—reiterated by Indian Shi'ites on the day of lamentation, when the defeat of Karbala is commemorated—gave rise to the Anglo-Indian expression *Hobson Jobson,* to denote a chaotic display of crowd sentiment.

25. Quoted in Taheri, *Holy Terror,* pp. 239–40.

4. GLOBALIZATION

1. Anna Geifman, *Thou Shalt Kill: Revolutionary Terrorism in Russia*, *1894–1917* (Princeton, N.J.: Princeton University Press, 1993).

2. The evidence for this judgment in the case of Iran can be found in Taheri, *Holy Terror.*

3. See again the account given by Bergen in *Holy War Inc.*

4. On some of the social and political effects of this, see Assef Bayat, *Street Politics: Poor People's Movements in Iran* (New York: Columbia University Press, 1997) and Diane Singerman, *Avenues of Participation: Family, Politics and Networks in Urban Quarters of Cairo* (Princeton, N.J.: Princeton University Press, 1995).

5. The point is forcefully made by Edward Mortimer, *Faith and Power,* p. 321.

6. On the terrorist origins of the PLO, see Jillian Becker,

The PLO: The Rise and Fall of the Palestine Liberation Organization (New York: St. Martin's), 1984.

7. Rosemary Righter, *Utopia Lost: The United Nations and World Order* (New York: Twentieth Century Fund Press, 1995).

8. See again Righter, *Utopia Lost,* and also, on a specific case, my *Who, What and Why?* a pamphlet published by the IEA (London, 2000).

9. See Michael Rowbotham, *Goodbye America!: Globalisation and the Debts of the Developing Nations* (London: Jon Carpenter, 2000).

10. Sir John Robert Seeley, *The Expansion of England in the Eighteenth Century* (London, 1883; Chicago, University of Chicago Press, 1971).

11. By the leftist author Thierry Meyssan, entitled *L'Effroyable Imposture: 11 septembre 2001* (Chatou: Carnot, 2002).

5. CONCLUSION

1. Geifman, *Thou Shalt Kill.*

INDEX